THE SUCCESS CODE

HOW ORDINARY HABITS CAN PRODUCE EXTRAORDINARY RESULTS

DAUNTLESS

CONTENTS

Contributors   v

Introduction   vii

1. PERSISTENCE WITH PURPOSE   1
Ray Brehm

2. THE POWER OF GRATITUDE   7
Marc Reklau

3. BE YOURSELF   13
Sierra Melcher

4. PATIENCE AND ADAPTATION   21
Louis A. Vendetti

5. THE POWER OF PERSEVERANCE   29
Catherine Chapman

6. THE CAREER SUCCESS CODE   35
Tony Pisanelli

7. WEALTH CO-CREATION   43
Clifford Todd

8. A 7-FIGURE BELIEF   51
Alinka Rutkowska

9. CREATE A BUSINESS THAT IS TRUE TO YOU   57
Karen Ferreira

10. SOMEDAY MAYBE - HARNESS YOUR TIME AND   63
ENERGY
Daniel Lee Smith

11. UNIQUE IDEAS HAVE THE POWER TO CHANGE   69
THE WORLD
Marie Incontrera

12. YOUR HEALTH CODE   75
Dr Marcus Chacos, chiropractor

13. YOUR "PLUS ONE"   83
Farhan A. Hamidani

14. HOW TO SUCCEED WITHOUT REALLY TRYING   91
Ange Hilstron

15. THE POWER OF THE PIVOT   97
    Paul Brodie

16. INTUITIVE DECISION MAKING   103
    Eric Todd Johnson, J.D., M.B.A.

17. NICELY SUCCESSFUL   109
    Lisa McNair Palmer, Esq.

18. RUN YOUR OWN RACE   115
    Leslie Olmo

19. STRENGTH-BASED SUCCESS   123
    Dr. Kanna Krishnan LLB Hons(Uk) MBA Hrm (Aus) DBA(Swit)

20. HABITUAL IMPLEMENTATION   129
    Brad Johnson

21. THE POWER OF VISION   137
    Barbara Miller

22. IN SYNC: THE KEY TO MAGNETIC SALES,   149
    BONDING CUSTOMER SERVICE, AND
    TRANSFORMATIVE LEARNING PROGRAMS
    Roy Varner

23. CODE YOUR MIND FOR SUCCESS   157
    Stephen Parr

24. MANIFEST THE LIFE YOU WANT   165
    Marie Temby

25. FIGHT THE COBRA   173
    Monica Rubombora

26. PASSIONIZE YOUR PERSONAL BRAND   185
    Sofia Jarlo

27. THE FLYING EAGLE FORMULA   193
    Deb Canja

28. A COMMITMENT TO GIVING   201
    Anthony Costa

    Join Us   209

CONTRIBUTORS

Ray Brehm, Marc Reklau, Sierra Melcher, Louis A. Vendetti, Catherine Chapman, Tony Pisanelli, Clifford Todd, Alinka Rutkowska, Karen Ferreira, Daniel Lee Smith, Marie Incontrera, Dr Marcus Chacos, chiropractor, Farhan A. Hamidani, Ange Hilstron, Paul Brodie, Eric Todd Johnson, J.D., M.B.A., Lisa McNair Palmer, Esq., Leslie Olmo, Dr. Kanna Krishnan LLB Hons(Uk) MBA Hrm(Aus) DBA(Swit), Brad Johnson, Barbara Miller, Roy Varner, Stephen Parr, Marie Temby, Monica Rubombora, Sofia Jarlo, Deb Canja, Anthony Costa

INTRODUCTION

The Success Code is a collection of life lessons. These are the habits, mindsets and stories of how the authors overcame obstacles and achieved success.

Some of these ideas focus on personal success, some focus on business success. But they all share the common theme of helping you realize your best self.

This book is a magnificent collection of authors from around the globe. For that reason, you will find some chapters written in American English and some in British English. In honor of our authors and the diversity of our global community, we intentionally chose to leave each chapter in its native version of English.

So fret not when you see words like "organize" and "organise" in subsequent chapters. We know the differences are there and we celebrate them.

We also celebrate you for picking up this book.

Our primary goal is to let you know, that if you are struggling, striving for more, or want to live the life of your dreams, you are in the right place.

You are not alone. What you are feeling is normal. There is nothing wrong with you.

You are simply on the lifelong path to building your personal success code.

We are so glad you are here.

Ray Brehm

1

PERSISTENCE WITH PURPOSE

RAY BREHM

It hit me like a ton of bricks, and I was not mentally prepared.

Have you ever been stopped in your tracks with despair? Or hit a wall, and wondered if you had peaked in your life?

I was feeling depression-like symptoms, which were not common feelings for me. I had always seen myself as a super positive person, with a "life is good" attitude. In fact, in my circles, I am well known for wearing Life Is Good® clothing.

So when I suddenly realized I was almost out of money and my dream career was not producing a positive cash flow, it was a new low. It was a combination of a dream dying and being all washed up at the same time.

I had recently sold my real estate business, convinced I had enough proof of concept in my author coaching and publishing business.

For about a year and a half, I burned the cash from the sale (like one of those dot com startups). I was sure a big pay day was right around the corner.

Except it wasn't.

Ignoring warnings from some business friends, I kept moving forward the same way, not changing anything I was doing.

Then, the third week of the month, I realized I didn't have enough money to pay all the bills for the following month.

That realization—along with some emotional personal events—triggered an almost instant change in state in my mind.

I was in a deep, dark place.

I suddenly couldn't even envision a future where I could pay the bills. My confidence in what I was doing was tossed out the window. For the first time in over a decade, I looked at the "Want Ads" for work (and wondered if I was qualified for anything listed).

I was deep in despair, and I didn't feel equipped to deal with it. I had no idea what to do.

Fortunately, my family was (and is) my rock. My wife had to keep me positive while watching me pace the kitchen every morning. Things may have been vastly different had she not been there.

I started reaching out to other entrepreneurs for guidance and support.

What I found was amazing: there was not one person I spoke with who had not experienced something similar, if not more dire—and more than once.

I kept reminding myself that this was something everyone, especially entrepreneurs, go through. It is part of the cycle.

Unfortunately, that knowledge alone was not doing it for me. I still felt extremely sad, and desperate.

It culminated with what I assume was a panic attack.

I was in the kitchen with my wife, describing some advice a friend of mine had given me. He had mentioned that we were still in a good spot, so why didn't we consider selling our house and buying an existing business?

The idea made a lot of sense, except that this was our home. It was our safe place, our fortress of solitude.

As I was explaining it, I suddenly got extremely nauseated and then very dizzy, all within seconds. I had to go over and put one hand on the couch to try not to throw up.

It passed, but I was miserable.

Then I called my long-time friend, Charlie Taylor. Not surprisingly, he had felt like that many times before.

Then he said something that made a huge difference.

"You have to break that cycle in your mind. You have to go outside, take a walk, and just look at nature."

I took my first walk a few hours later.

At the same time, there was a Tony Robbins / Dean Graziosi webinar going on. I figured watching it might help a little.

They talked about how overnight success is rarely overnight. Actually, persistence is what normally separates successful entrepreneurs from the rest.

Though still very deep down, a part of me realized I already had the tools to combat my mind and emotions.

The dark side of my mind was telling me I had blown it. I had blown my money, I would never make another dollar online, and I would have to get a job I was sure to hate.

My dark side was winning, but the battle wasn't over.

So I started with baby steps.

I had learned affirmations and visualizations from Hal Elrod and Jack Canfield. I knew I needed to break the cycle of my dark side, and I knew that success takes time.

The whole time I was in this dark place, quitting felt like the easiest thing to do—except there was nowhere to quit to.

Any job I might be able to acquire would barely pay as much as I was already making. It was just a security blanket that would trap me.

So, I decided what I needed to do was affirm something in my mind. Every moment I felt the extreme dark side, especially when I woke up in the middle of the night, I said this to myself:

I am worthy.
I am wealthy.
I live an abundant life.

I have said it ever since. In the years that followed, I have also added:

We are debt-free.

We have an eight-figure company.

That next day, I meditated five times. The day after, four times. I took walks and I was constantly telling myself the above affirmations.

I was extremely persistent about it. I had no idea how it would all work out, or how I would feel better, but I continued to do those three things:

1. Break the cycle
2. Affirmations
3. Meditations

I remember still feeling down the next ten to fourteen days, but each day I started to feel a little better.

During this period, I was interviewing people I really admired for an upcoming summit I was hosting. I remember being so depressed, and then having to make sure I got myself "up" for the interviews.

I don't believe anyone ever suspected anything was wrong. In fact, I believe I started fooling myself as well (in a good way).

Then a funny thing happened.

I started to make money. I started to feel success.

And I suddenly realized the dark side wasn't there any longer.

Less than forty-five days from the start of my downward spiral, I made more money than I had the entire prior year.

The money was not the end goal, of course, but confidence was, and that income gave me confidence in myself and in my dream business.

Obviously, I already had a business when all this started. But I was ready to throw it away.

The universe was, in a sense, telling me to get my ducks in a row. I had to refocus my mind and run it like a business. I would no longer throw bad money after good, rather choosing to just connect and serve those I was meant to serve.

I recently started watching a reality series on The History

Channel called Alone. This is a show where ten contestants are left alone in the wilderness. The last one to quit wins 500k.

After watching a season or two, you will quickly realize that hunting or survival skills, while important, do not equal winning.

It is a mind game. Those who can endure the loneliness, guilt, and days of depression last the longest.

Season Two was won by a guy named David McIntyre.

He said something really profound:

"There is value in suffering."

I know the cliche, "you don't know how good the good times are without the bad." And while I agree, that is not the main point.

The "down times" create the skills needed for life. The "bad times" create skills needed for the next down time.

Pain is never easy. Fighting the dark side of your mind is never easy.

And persistence is definitely not easy.

But when you realize you have come out of a dark time through persistence, it is priceless and wonderful.

To quote Tim Allen's character Jason Nesmith of Galaxy Quest, "Never give up. Never Surrender."

You can reach Ray at raybrehm.com.

2

THE POWER OF GRATITUDE

MARC REKLAU

If you heard me speak, saw an interview with me, or read any of my books, you know that one of my favorite success habits that I recommend to everybody and apply myself is gratitude. If there is any "secret" to my success, it's definitely the "Power of Gratitude."

When you ask me what the difference between selling eight books a month and 5000 books a month on Amazon is, then the answer will most probably be the "Power of Gratitude," meaning the constant state of gratitude I'm in.

What does that mean? It means being grateful for all the good things you have in your life, the good things that happen to you every day, and even the good things that are on the way to you but not in your life yet. There are so many things in your life that you can be grateful for. Unfortunately - if you are like most people - you probably take them for granted or are so busy doing other things all the time that you even forget about them.

Why gratitude? Because it's one of the most powerful forces in the universe. Gratitude brings good things into your life and makes you notice more of the good things you already have.

Careful now! Practicing gratitude doesn't mean being grateful

once a year or every now and then. It means making practicing gratitude a daily habit, or even better a lifestyle.

Gratitude has changed my life completely. I went from jobless to
an international bestselling author who has sold over 350.000 books
in a bit more than six years. I left behind a lot of toxic relationships,
and my relationships - personal and business - are now healthy and
well. Of course, there were other habits involved in getting me there.
Still, after a lot of thinking and reflecting, I concluded that the main
factor for the fantastic changes in my life—and one of the primary
ingredients for my success—is gratitude. The more grateful I became
in my life—without expecting anything in exchange—the better and
more successful my life became.

So how does it work? Easy. Every day write down at least three
things that you are grateful for. No. Don't make the exercise in your
head; don't just think about the three things. Write them down!

Here's what I wrote down on November 11, 2013, the day I started
my gratitude practice:

I'm grateful that I'm alive.
I'm grateful for my family.
I'm grateful for my friends who support me.
I'm grateful for the cup of coffee I had at the beach bar.
I'm grateful for working hard.
I'm grateful for that good lunch that I had with a friend.
I'm grateful for that good presentation I attended.
I'm grateful for a sunny day.

Okay, that's more than three ...

It's also important that you FEEL the gratitude with every cell of
your body. It seems that gratitude works better when you put a lot of
emotion into it. This is important, so I'll repeat it: *Gratitude works best
when it comes from the heart, and you feel the gratitude.*

Gratitude really changes everything. Once you seriously start
practicing gratitude, you'll see your world in an entirely different way,
and everything will begin to change. When you are grateful, this

universal energy responds by giving you more things to be grateful for. Call it focus, call it energy. I can't fully explain how it works, but man does it work! It seems like God, life, the universe, or destiny (choose whatever you prefer) says, "Look at you! You're happy with everything you have in your life. Let's give you more."

What can you be grateful for? Let's see. What about your parents, your friends, your health? Do you appreciate every breath you take, every flower you see on your way, your friends' company? If not, NOW would be a good time to start!

Writing down three things, you're grateful for every day to change your life? Come on! I really can't make it a lot easier for you! The most important thing is to start. Remember, it's all a matter of practice, so give yourself time. Don't be too demanding, and above all, don't beat yourself up if you don't see results right away.

Gratitude is the best antidote to all the negative emotions. Did you ever notice that you can't feel negative emotions while you practice gratitude? You can't feel any kind of worry, anger, or depression while you practice gratitude. You can't even get upset about your current life circumstances while you're practicing gratitude. You can't be grateful and unhappy at the same time. You can't be grateful and worried at the same time. You can't be grateful and angry at the same time.

But don't take my word for it. It's scientifically proven that gratitude improves your life. All you have to do is write down three things you are grateful for every day for the next six to eight weeks (and feel the gratitude), and your life will change for the better. Really. Just do it! The results will be awesome, and your life will never be the same.

Prosperity is often just around the corner. Many people are practicing the principles and habits of success but stay stuck or poor. Something is blocking them from success. It could be a lack of forgiveness, but often the only reason for it is a lack of gratitude.

Don't give up if things don't go smoothly at first. It needs some time, but slowly, you'll get better and better at it thanks to the magic of discipline and repetition. If you need additional motivation, remember that science has proven that doing your gratitude exercises every day after four to six weeks *will* create amazing results. For example, better sleep, better mood, more optimism, a better social life, seeing more opportunities, having fewer headaches, being less prone to depression, and a lot more. This stuff really works.

You should have five minutes a day to do these exercises no matter what your situation is. Tony Robbins once said, "If you don't have five minutes a day, you don't have a life."

I'll repeat it once more because it can't be said often enough: being grateful rewires your brain to see more of the positive things that are around you. You will see more opportunities, and you will see open doors for you where there wasn't even a door before. When you are grateful for what you have, more things that you can be grateful for will come into your life. So be grateful for what you have and even for the things you don't have yet.

Sometimes, when you're going through a rough patch, it might be challenging to be grateful, I know. But believe me, there is always something to be grateful for, such as you, your body, your talents, your friends, your family, or nature. Start small. When I was jobless, I was grateful for drinking a cup of coffee in the sun, having a good night's sleep, and having friends. Instead of starting your day by complaining about what you don't have or dreading what is to come, start it by saying thank you for what you have. Focus on everything that's going well for you.

Stop comparing. Practice gratitude instead. Count your blessings instead of other people's blessings. This exercise alone can probably "cure" you of jealousy and envy if you practice it for three to four weeks.

The more I practice gratitude, the sweeter my day gets. I get up from my computer various times a day, go out, take a short five- to fifteen-minute walk, and feel gratitude. Feel the gratitude just after waking up and just before going to sleep. The first half an hour of your day sets the tone for the rest of your day. The last half an hour of your day is also critical. What you feed your brain at that time will keep vibrating during your sleep. It's these two times when your subconscious mind is the most active and most receptive. So feed your brain gratitude.

Remember, your perception shapes your reality. Focusing on the positive can dramatically improve your success. This has been proven over and over again. Be patient, be consistent, and you will succeed.

Gratitude is not a magic pill, although it certainly has all the ingredients. Once you do the work in the real world, magic happens. I wish you this magic and now go and write down three things you are grateful for today!

You can reach Marc at marcreklau.com.

3

BE YOURSELF

SIERRA MELCHER

In college, I thought I had to save the world. What's more, I believed I had to do it single-handedly. I had thrown myself so deeply into building an organization that I had lost any sense of myself outside of what I was creating. As you can imagine, I drove myself into a frenzy and lived on the edge of burnout. This ragged state led me to wonder: **What if the only thing I *had* to do in the world was be myself?**

Be myself? I'm not sure I had been a person at all. I was a walking idea, a force of nature. If my efforts failed, *I* failed. I had lost any sense of self; I had no idea who I was if I wasn't my accomplishments. This state was untenable—however, I would continue to make variations of this same mistake for years.

I spent fifteen years as an international educator, teaching in high schools around the world. I loved the work, but it took a disproportionate toll on my health and wellbeing. Craving more challenge and flexibility, I opened a bilingual yoga studio in Medellin, Colombia. I ended up selling it a few years later as a thriving Mecca of innovative learning and practice. Although it was great, it wasn't great *for me*.

What if the common wisdom was wrong?

My favorite book as a child tells of a young woman whose grandfather taught her three things to live a good life: he said, "travel the world, grow old by the sea, and make the world more beautiful." I traveled the world, and I have yet to grow old, so the granddaughter in the story and I both focused on wondering how to make the world a more beautiful place.

As humans, we are trying to live our dream and contribute in a meaningful way to the world. My attempts took an immeasurable toll on me. I followed the conventional wisdom, chased all the shiny things. All the advice and so-called "wisdom" led me to a place of horrible discontent. I poured everything into work, but at the cost of myself.

For years, I lived in this misalignment, believing that I just needed to work harder, work smarter, take another class, and *then* I would figure it out. It took the birth of my daughter to show me that I was looking for answers in all the wrong places. Now, rather than being misaligned, I am Ms. Aligned.

Being pregnant and giving birth connected me with my body and intuition in a way I had never experienced before. This growing connection threw me into a powerful relationship with myself that taught me more than I ever imagined, with a few vital breakdowns along the way. I began to seek answers in a new way and in a new place. I have been on a journey ever since.

Clients come to me because something that used to work for them or feel fulfilling to them no longer works. They come with discomfort or crisis. I am now so grateful for my various struggles because I am now more equipped to support others, having been there myself. Often, we know we are uncomfortable but are not sure what to do about it. I want to share with you the fundamental perspective shift I teach my clients, which both optimizes and accelerates growth. That is my zone of genius.

We crave the breakthrough, the moment when everything clicks.

We all want the "Aha" moment when everything aligns. And we have all had them. What we forget is what got us there.

Breakdown

Maybe a breakdown manifests in your business itself, in your health, or in your relationship. Wherever it occurs, the unifying characteristic of a breakdown is that you can't miss it. It will stop you in your tracks. While there may have been signs it was coming, you resisted them until you no longer could.

This is a hard place to be, yet we make it harder by viewing a breakdown in negative terms.

What if a breakdown, a crisis, a collapse, was the richest opportunity for growth?

- Would you feel differently about it?
- What if you reframe this idea, and change your mindset?

It is not a breakdown. It's a *break-down-through.*

Tell me you don't want that moment: "I've figured it out, it feels so great!"

I want a breakthrough. We all want a breakthrough! But I have never had a breakthrough without at least visiting, if not spending way too much time in, breakdown.

Next time you are in crisis, thinking, "Everything is falling apart!" think instead, "Congratulations!" You have arrived at the place just before your next destination, your breakthrough.

Breakdowns can lead to breakthroughs.

Crisis is a fundamental stage of growth, and it is a sign you are on the right track! It means you are growing and have likely outgrown the current and familiar container. You are ready for more. But you need to go further into discomfort, further into the unknown, further into the breakdown, which we are all so resistant to do. That is where the deepest learning is, where the "Aha" moments live, and where your next success resides.

No one goes here for fun. When staying in the familiar is so uncomfortable that you can't stay any longer, only *then* will you be willing. My mentor, Dr. Onani Carver, explains it like a chick in an egg. At the beginning, that eggshell is vital, a protective container. Little by little, the embryo grows until it has reached the limits of that shell. Now it needs more food and more space. It has to break the shell and abandon the very thing that protected it thus far. To stay in the familiarity of the shell is to die. As humans, this is an existential crisis. But the chick, emerging from the shell, doesn't look too perturbed.

Humans, with all our judgments and massive brains, sometimes get in our *own* way. When we have outgrown the protective container of one phase, we are often terrified to break out of it. Only when we can no longer tolerate the pain or discomfort of misalignment are we willing to go into the unknown, to evolve in our business or personal lives. Our resistance to growth is a real detriment.

Break-Down-Through

A friend of mine is a neuroscientist, (isn't that cool? a real neuroscientist!). "Fail fast" is an expression she and her colleagues hold dear. Rather than trying to be right and spend ages trying to prove it, neuroscientists aspire to be *wrong* as fast as possible, to drop a false lead and seek a new one. This philosophy embodies what I teach my clients about the beauty of a *break-down-through*.

There is nothing more successful, more human, that learning and growing. This happens at every age. Our struggles are a sign of our progress, but most of us have that backward. We begrudge our struggles, we try to make it work by trying harder. We want an easy triumph, without growing or learning our lessons.

So much of individual and systemic suffering comes from being disconnected from ourselves and one another. We are unhappy because we have been following a prescribed path that we unwittingly adopted, trusting that it would yield us promised results. However, while it may have worked for someone, it didn't work for us. It is tragic to spend your precious time, energy, and money on something that does not serve you. There is bound to be conflict when we are striving for a goal that was never truly ours. It often takes a breakdown to clue us in. When we do not fundamentally know who we are, how can we possibly build meaningful relationships in our personal life or in our business?

I want to make clear an important distinction: learning and growing *is* success! There will inevitably be things we need to learn and people or sources we will turn to to learn both about our business and our life. This is not about learning. What I am talking about is more fundamental. What got us stuck was *unconsciousness*.

In life, as in business, outsourcing your authority is futile; you will never be happy, no matter how hard you try, if you are disconnected. Distinguishing between learning and abdicating your vital choice is a very personal process. The deep work is waking up to massive misalignment and charting a new, conscious course. It's a realization that each of us can choose and create a life that is fulfilling. When we are not autonomous, we will live abiding by the learned dictations of what we *should* want, how we *should* live, and what a "successful life" is supposed to look like.

For me, being in business has been the most intense personal discovery journey thus far. Entrepreneurism has uncovered many places where I was operating on autopilot, only to arrive at my destination without any sense of meaning or accomplishment. We have far more capacity in our lives than we believe, and thus more responsibility to live it well.

For years I was there, in the struggle. Now, I teach people how to be their *own* guru and find the answers *within,* in work, in relationships, in all things. I believe in a world where people own the power of their own decisions and no longer give that right to others, intentionally or unconsciously. I am on a mission to create a new paradigm where the ultimate authority is found within each of us. I guide leaders and change-makers to discover this realization for themselves so the powerful impact they have on the world fuels them, in their heart and soul.

I don't want another person to spend a minute longer in their own way because they believe they have to "do the right thing" (i.e. stay in a marriage or a job that is crippling their soul, or just not right for them). When we are not connected to ourselves, we are living in someone else's story. Our lives are not truly our own. We cannot thrive or approach fulfillment when we are not fundamentally engaged in our own lives.

I guide people to untangle the external messaging, to discover the true self with a clear process, but I cannot do it for them. As in myths, every great hero must go into the labyrinth on their own, slay the demon, and emerge triumphant on their own account. No one can discover your ultimate authority for you. You have to do it yourself.

However, just as heroes all have mentors, it is essential to have a guide by your side.

Here are a few ideas to get you started on **discovering & deepening your ultimate authority from within:**

- **Accountability** *(to self)*- Listen deeply and tune-in to know yourself better and to distinguish external dictations from inner wisdom.
- **Alignment** *(with self)*- recalibrate to work in and for your highest potential.
- **Agency** *(for self)*- know you have the capacity to remake your life based on your true self and aligned desires.
- **Authenticity** *(of self)*- integrate the action and expression of who you are and what you believe in, even when it is imperfect or messy.

Be Your Messy Self

There must be room for you, the person, the author of your own story, in your business and in your life. If you are working so hard that you lose yourself and or you are not able to be kind and connected, you have lost the magic. Let your next breakdown be an invitation to a success yet to come. Human connection is vital, and we are magnetized to energetic, aligned people who are happy—because that is what we all seek. Be that person for yourself and for others.

So, whatever your business, be in the business of being yourself. Discover who you are and be that person *fiercely*. This is what the world, and you, need most. What's good for you *is* good for business!

If what I have shared here resonates with you, if this has been helpful, if you are inspired to realign, I would be thrilled to hear from you.

Visit https://integral-women.mykajabi.com/.

4

PATIENCE AND ADAPTATION

LOUIS A. VENDETTI

What is success? Outwardly it is often measured by how wealthy someone is, but wealth itself is not success. It is, though, sometimes a byproduct of success.

An annual favorite movie in our house is the Frank Capra movie, *It's a Wonderful Life* with Jimmy Stewart. In the movie, George Bailey (Stewart) never realized his dream of leaving his hometown to see the world and build skyscrapers due to his obligations, but in the end, his hometown helped him out of a jam and declared him "the richest man in town." Here was a man with no financial success, but he definitely lived a successful life.

You have to decide what success means to you.

When I was younger, I wanted to be like George Bailey: a man who helped others. So I went through the usual occupations that most young kids dream about—EMT, fireman, policeman. I even earned my First Aid, CPR, and AED certification when I was in my junior year of high school. However, when it came time to recertify, I was told the guidelines for certification were changed. It was no longer something I could pursue, due to my Cerebral Palsy and inability to stand without assistance.

In the years since my certification lapsed, I found other passions.

Some of them were rekindled from when I was younger; others were found as I was getting ready to go off to college. All of them got me to where I am today, either directly or indirectly.

One thing that always interested me was writing. In my freshman year of high school, I had an English teacher who pushed me to make my writing better. He nurtured in me my love of writing. In my first writing assignment, he commented that my writing skills were a double-edged sword: they got me a great grade, but he was going to be expecting more from me throughout the duration of the school year. That was a challenge I eagerly accepted!

Throughout the class, we read and analyzed many books and movies. One of my favorite books was *Tuesdays with Morrie* by Mitch Albom. In the book, Albom speaks about his time in college when he had a professor who changed his career, named Morrie Schwartz.

After Albom saw his former professor being interviewed on "Nightline" with Ted Koppel, he flew down to reunite with him. Eventually, Albom went down there on a weekly basis for interviews.

What came from those weekly Tuesday interviews was the book *Tuesdays with Morrie*, where Albom chronicles Schwartz's life and the wisdom that he wants to impart on the world after he passes away. Schwartz was diagnosed with Amyotrophic Lateral Sclerosis (ALS), also known as Lou Gehrig's disease, which caused a slow death. As Schwartz was being interviewed, as Albom chronicles in the book, you could see the toll the disease was having on his body.

On the seventh Tuesday visit Albom had with Schwartz, Schwartz speaks about dependency:

I'm an independent person, so my inclination was to fight all of this —being helped from the car, having someone else dress me. I felt a little ashamed, because our culture tells us we should be ashamed if we can't wipe our own behind . . .

And you know what? The strangest thing.

I began to *enjoy* my dependency. Now I enjoy when they turn me over on my side and rub cream on my behind so I don't get sores. Or when they wipe my brow, or they massage my legs. I revel in it. I close my eyes and soak it up. And it seems very familiar to me.

It's like going back to being a child again. Someone to bathe you. Someone to lift you. Someone to wipe you. We all know how to be a child. It's inside all of us. For me, it's just remembering how to enjoy it.

The truth is, when our mothers held us, rocked us, stroked our heads—none of us ever got enough of that. We all yearn in some way to return to those days when we were completely taken care of —unconditional love, unconditional attention. Most of us didn't get enough. (Albom 109-110)[1]

Granted, his form of dependence and mine are two totally different things, but this book really spoke to me. Due to my Cerebral Palsy, I may need help with some things I cannot physically do, but that doesn't mean I cannot be successful. Success is not measured by being able-bodied.

At around this same time, I found a story I had written when I was ten years old. On it I had also written the goal of being an author by the age of twenty. During the time between finding that and when I published my first book, I had a lot of things other good things happen. Some of the most notable were that I graduated high school and went onto college, was inducted into Phi Theta Kappa—the fraternity for two-year colleges—and graduated from my alma mater with honors.

The whole process of writing and publishing my first book was far more complicated than I thought. As the days turned into weeks, the weeks into months, and the months into a year and a half in business, I've realized there are three ingredients for success.

1. Success takes time and willingness to adapt
2. Success takes dedication and hard work
3. Success takes planning and goal setting

Success Takes Time and Willingness to Adapt

We have all heard of overnight successes. A movie someone starred in tops the box office charts, a song hits the top of the charts—but, when you look into the actor's or songwriter's backstories, you will see that they are not the overnight success they appear to be. It took them years of hard work to get to where they are.

For me, the publishing of my first book, *My Disability Doesn't Define Me*, took longer than I expected. Little did I know that the writing of the book was the easy part. The business of getting it published was much more complicated.

When 2019 ended, I vowed to myself that 2020 would be the year that changed my life—and business—forever, so I made provisions to make sure this happened.

At the beginning of 2020, I found my good friend, Ray, had put together another Co-Author Project book, so I jumped at the opportunity to be part of it (that project culminated into the book that you're reading right now!). That's just one of the exciting things that happened.

I went on to work on publishing other books (including co-authoring a few more books with my friend Ray) and I started putting my name out to a few podcasts to see if they'd be willing to have me on as a guest. I was slowly starting to make a name for myself.

I also went on to create packages to help clients publish their own books, as well as a full-service publishing package!

Here I was, thinking that I would only publish my own books—instead, it sort of "snowballed" into other areas. I certainly didn't expect it by any means, but life has a way of taking you in unexpected directions. You need to be open to opportunities and not be afraid of stepping into the unknown.

I came to realize that, by being impatient, by picturing myself successful in a certain way, I was pigeonholing myself and limiting my potential. The original direction was to publish my own books for the duration of my business life, but it has turned into so much more. Now, along with publishing my own books, I started helping others publish theirs. I am also co-authoring books and helping others with their websites and email marketing—who knows where it will end!

Success Takes Dedication and Hard Work

You often hear that someone's success is due to their being lucky. This is another myth, like being an overnight success. Being successful takes dedication and hard work. On any given day, I'm up from 9 a.m. to 3 a.m. Sometimes I don't really sleep at all, though I usually do get a cat nap in!

Since I'm a one-man show, I am my marketing department, my PR department, my HR department, as well as my sales department. Usually, I'm up working on my writing or maybe a new project that I want to create and promote well into the night and next morning.

Creating my publishing packages is an example. I was recently on a social networking site and saw someone ask a question about writing a book. So, I reached out to them and we scheduled a time for a pre-publishing call.

Between the time that I spoke with them and the appointment time, I was up all hours of the night trying to figure out what I was going to offer in the packages and then how to price each package. With this, I expanded my business to include assisting others write and publish their books.

However, I didn't just create the packages and sit back to wait for people to come after them. This is *not* "I will create it and they will come." That's not what business is about. Just because you create something *doesn't* mean people will automatically come and buy it. You have to network with people. You have to advertise your products and/or services. At some points, you may find yourself having to go out there and hustle for the business, like I had to.

If you do not go out and network with people, you are missing out on key business opportunities and partnerships that could have been the key to your success. If you do not market your business, your products, or your services, no one will buy them—simply because they don't know they're there.

Depending on the type of marketing that you do in your business, you may not see new leads overnight; it may take a while. Organic marketing—for example, getting out there and posting on Facebook or utilizing your mailing list—takes a while.

Email marketing is a great form of organic marketing. Your list is composed of your customers—the people who enjoy your work, your fans. These are people who will potentially buy from you at some point in time, or are people who have bought from you in the past.

My business, my opportunities, weren't handed to me—and yours won't be handed to you. You need to recognize opportunities when they come along and act on them. When the Coronavirus pandemic started to take over our lives and we were told to socially isolate for the foreseeable future in order to help stop the spread, I thought, *Why not create a writing project to help everyone stay productive in this time of social isolation?*

Hopefully, some talented, aspiring writers will see the writing project, recognize the opportunity, and act on it.

Success Takes Planning and Goal Setting

The final myth is that some people are just successful and others aren't, as if something outside of our control decides who is successful and who is not. We control what we become, and in order to be successful you need a plan and you need to articulate and work toward your goals.

We all have things we want to achieve, and those are sometimes considered our "big goals" (which are great to have!), but how will you accomplish those big goals?

In order to accomplish bigger goals, you need to break your bigger goals down into smaller chunks. My goal setting worksheet will help you with this.

Please go here to download it: https://louisvendetti.com/the-success-code-goal-worksheet.

The goal worksheet is from a book that I have in development. In it, I speak about achieving your goals in greater detail. If you'd like to stay up to date about my upcoming releases and other projects, you can join my newsletter by downloading the worksheet above.

I look forward to hearing how you prosper while using the template!

To connect with Louis https://louisvendetti.com.

---

1. Albom, Mitch. *Tuesdays with Morrie*, Broadway Books, 1997, 2017: pp. 109-110.

5

THE POWER OF PERSEVERANCE

CATHERINE CHAPMAN

The most important aspect of success for me was perseverance. My story begins in 1990, a lifetime ago. I had two small children.

I was a typical mum who wanted her kids to eat healthy. Unfortunately, this was difficult because fast food was becoming really popular and was such a novelty. Our kids were enticed by the fast food companies, with their fun characters and toys that came free with their meals.

Parents had to battle to convince their kids that they should be eating more fruit and vegetables. Sadly, fast forward to today and not much has changed. In fact, there are more fast food places than ever.

It was a worry for me. My husband and his family had a history of diabetes, which meant my children had a fifty percent chance of becoming diabetic. It was up to me as a parent to try to avoid the possibility of my children suffering from a disease that is largely preventable.

I knew that my husband's condition, type 2 diabetes, was largely due to lifestyle and eating habits. I wanted to give my children the best chance I could of avoiding type 2 diabetes, and I knew that their diet would play a major role in preventing it. I also knew that giving my children the tools to eating healthy would help them control their diabetes if they were unfortunate enough to inherit the disease.

I tried bribery and then I tried forcing them to eat their fruit and veggies, both to no avail. I was so fed up with trying. Then, one night, I had an idea. I thought about how the fast food companies offered toys and fun characters to get kids to eat unhealthy food. Why not create some characters that instil a "healthy eating" message? What if I created some little characters that were fruit and vegetables and got the kids to like them? Then I could use them to get the kids to like the fruit or vegetable the character represented.

I began to draw some fun characters. As I was drawing, my son called me into his room and asked me to read him a story. While reading, the whole concept came to me. It was like a movie streaming from the bedroom window. I saw books with characters and my name on them. I saw a bookcase, plates, and bedspreads. The characters had personalities and I could see what they looked like. Was this a vision? I believe it was, and that the whole thing was given to me.

That night, I sat down and wrote ten stories about ten characters. It was effortless. The stories just came to me. The next day, I introduced the concept to my children. They loved the characters, and they made it easy for me to talk about healthy eating. Before long, they were asking for fruit and vegetables in the supermarket and relating the different fruit and vegetables to the characters.

I took the books to their school when I volunteered to read to the class. I read them to the children and the teachers. Everyone loved the stories and the teacher asked me to bring them in each week.

I read them to family and friends and they suggested I try to get the stories published. So I did. It was 1990 and there was a recession in Australia. I sent the books to several publishers. A few copies were returned with the comment, "Dear Catherine, your stories are delightful, however due to the fact that we are in recession the concept of publishing ten books is not something we could do at this time."

Some publishers did not even bother to return the books. My excitement turned to disappointment. The recession was hard for everyone in Australia. I just got on with my life. My kids still loved to have the stories read to them and I had found a way to teach them about fruit and vegetables through these fun characters. As time marched on, my kids outgrew the stories and I put the books away in my garage.

Fast forward to 2007. I found my books again while cleaning out the garage. Remembering how much the books helped my own children learn how to eat healthy and appreciate healthy food, I decided to try again, as the world was waking up to the fact that unhealthy food was causing disease and fruit and vegetables were really important in our diet. I decided to search the internet and look for a co-author, maybe someone with a nutritional background. Big mistake. I was taken for a ride by a professional con artist. That mistake cost me over $30,000.00. It was devastating, to say the least, so I will leave that story for another chapter as it is too painful to think about.

I didn't want to give up, because in my heart I knew how good the characters were and how much they had helped my own kids.

I was doing some charity work with diabetes when the marketing manager asked if I could help raise funds through schools by using my characters and supplying some merchandise. I organised to have bag tags with the characters on them to hang on the kids' school bags to remind them to eat healthy. We supplied packs of stickers to sell in the supermarkets. Parents could purchase them and the money would go to the charity. We also took the merchandise to schools and gave the books to the libraries.

While this was successful, it was mainly all for charity, as I was so intent on introducing the characters to kids at school. Before long, thousands of kids were exposed to the characters. I had life-sized characters made up and the kids loved them—the parents and teachers did, too. Many parents asked me for car stickers and other merchandise with the characters on them. Unfortunately, financially, this was something I was unable to fund. I had spent a considerable amount already on the merchandise and books for the charity.

The characters toured schools for several years with a hip-hop dance company. It was a lot of fun and made a big impact on the kids.

In 2013, I decided to show the books at one of the children's book fairs in Shanghai. I couldn't believe the reception I received. Publishers were taking photos of the characters and asking me to consider publishing with them.

Then, the organisers of the book fair wanted to have the rights to the characters and all the books. They made me a substantial offer. There were offers coming from everywhere, but I decided to go with the organisers, as they were a large publishing house in China.

They were not publishing children's books yet—they currently published for schools and universities—but they wanted to expand into the children's book industry. After seeing my characters, they wanted to publish my books and use my characters in schools to help educate Chinese children, as diabetes was a major disease in China. We discussed merchandise and school tours. They sent the president of their company to meet me. It was all very exciting.

When I arrived back in Australia, I contacted my lawyer, who drafted a contract. China sent a Memorandum of Understanding (MOU). In most countries, an MOU is a binding document and you need to follow through after stamping and signing it.

It was around Christmas time and China closed down for the New Year. All of a sudden, I did not hear from them. When they returned back after a few months, they sent me an apology letter saying they were unable to go ahead with the contract, as they had decided to turn their company into a print-on-demand publishing house. Once more, I was devastated. I thought about how stupid I had been to choose them when so many other publishers were interested in my books and characters.

Fortunately, I had all my books listed with an agency in China and I was eventually contacted by another publisher, who wanted a five-year contract to sell the books. They printed half in English and half in Chinese. They paid me up front and immediately printed six thousand copies per title. That came to forty-two thousand copies.

My patience and perseverance paid off. I was an internationally published author. My books were in print and selling in China!

I now wanted to find a way to share the characters with kids everywhere in the world, so I published the books on Amazon and Apple. I also wrote some fun recipe books turning unhealthy food into healthy food.

Now is an exciting time for me, as I am happy knowing kids everywhere can access my books and benefit from having a best "food friend" in their life.

The books are not designed for kids to read alone. They are designed for parents to read to their children. Each character has its own personality, and the book is based on the personality of the character rather than on healthy eating.

The aim is for the kids to fall in love with the character and, in turn, relate the character to the healthy fruit or vegetable it represents. This then leads the kids to ask for healthy food. The characters give parents an opportunity to talk to their children about healthy food using the characters as examples.

Future generations need to know how to eat well in a fast food world. Unfortunately, fast food is not going away. Actually, it is increasing, as people become busier and have less time to prepare healthy food.

While the occasional take-out dinner is fine, living by the 80/20 rule—that is, 80% healthy and 20% occasional, unhealthy foods—will give your children a better start in life and better chance of not getting serious diseases like diabetes, heart disease, and obesity (which are all preventable).

So, there you have it. For me, success is a journey, not a destination. Even though throughout my journey I persevered and had success, the journey is not over. There are plenty more success stories from Best Food Friends still to come.

You can reach Catherine at www.bestfoodfriends.com

6

THE CAREER SUCCESS CODE

TONY PISANELLI

Back in March 2020, I received a phone call from a young gentleman in his mid-twenties named Dylan. He introduced himself by saying that he worked for an organization that supports the intellectually disabled, through which he knew my younger brother, Vincent. The reason for his phone call was to see if I was interested in hiring him to coordinate support services for my brother during the Coronavirus lockdown period.

Within minutes of this call, it became obvious that, for Dylan, being able to serve my brother meant more than simply keeping his job and income at a time when thousands were losing theirs. The enthusiasm in his voice and his connection to my brother made the decision easy. I hired him to support Vincent through the indefinite closure of his training facility.

During our phone conversations, while we arranged alternate support services, I was impressed by his commitment to deal with a complex system with constantly changing rules and approval parameters, all while working under tight budgetary discipline.

Dylan's workday constantly went above and beyond simply performing a set of routine tasks during the normal nine to five standard hours. He actively listened to understand the deeper picture behind our home life, my brother's personal challenges, and my situation as his carer. Also, he did not just recommend and organize service providers but also followed up to make sure our needs were satisfied.

I knew his deep devotion toward my brother and attitude to his work did not happen by chance. Clearly, there were important life experiences driving his commitment, and I was determined to learn his story.

He agreed to share his journey late one Friday evening, when others may have turned their attention to weekend recreation. During this call, he shared how he had commenced his career as a call centre employee, selling technology and telecommunication services to home customers. This career choice had been motivated by Steve Jobs, who was Dylan's iconic hero in his teenage years.

He recalled how he travelled to work on his first day with a spring in his step, overflowing with enthusiasm and energy as he sought in his own way to emulate the feats of his hero.

Like all hero stories, he encountered a villain that sought to spoil his "*apple* cart," so to speak. This villain was an organizational environment where people were treated like numbers, were undervalued, and were held to unrealistic performance expectations. The team he worked in referred to themselves as the telephone monkeys, a name that reflected how the company attempted to dehumanize them, prohibited communication between staff, and sought to turn them into super-efficient, scripted robots.

This was a long way off Dylan's definition of a high-performance culture which was the way the company had portrayed itself in the job advertisement that he had applied for.

By the end of the first week in the job, it had become clear that this position had a short use by date. He tolerated these circumstances because he knew that it was a role that would develop his resilience in dealing with and bouncing back from hard knocks. He also believed the job was a training ground for developing his business and technology acumen that would serve both his career and life.

The day that almost crushed his spirit and saw him walk out the door for good was when he arrived to work forty-five minutes late. His manager called Dylan behind closed doors and tore him to shreds because he had thrown out the staff roster and hurt the team's service and productivity performance. Dylan's explanation—that his home had been burgled—received no sympathy from his manager.

"They don't care about us. They only care about achieving performance metrics," Dylan cried to his fellow workmates.

The company's attitude clearly didn't sit well with Dylan, as he was someone who placed considerable importance on caring for people and creating a sense of family. This was a quality instilled by his parents, who frequently opened their home to children and young people, offering them stability and security, through foster care.

The call centre was certainly not the family dynamic he was used to. He decided to depart that role when his contract expired. When he told his manager of his decision to leave, the manager expressed his reluctance to letting him go and wanted to know why, as Dylan was a bright future prospect with team-leading abilities.

His response was lifted straight from the well-known advice given by Steve Jobs to Steve Wozniak: "Do you want to sell sugar water all your life, or do you want to come with me and change the world?"

The words that kept reverberating in Dylan's mind were, "Do I want to sell technology for the rest of my life and be treated as a cheap commodity or do I want to make a difference in people's lives by expressing who I am deep inside?"

Feeling a strong pull toward a career path that integrated people and family values and given the absence of responsibilities and obligations at this stage of his life, made his decision to leave relatively easy.

During our Friday night conversation, Dylan shared the story of his close and deep relationship with his cousin Robbie who had cerebral palsy. Dylan became very emotional and choked on his words when he shared that Robbie had died from the condition at the tender age of eighteen.

I could now see why Dylan wanted to make a difference in the lives' of people with a disability. I was also keen to know how he came about securing this role as a carer, when his only prior work experience was technology. Dylan was surprised and delighted to have been shortlisted for an interview, given the fact that his work history fell well short of the position's job description. What Dylan found out later was a little bird named Brittney had whispered in the recruiter's ear about the quality of his character. This became a pivotal moment when his resume was moved from the "maybe later pile" to the definite interview" basket.

At the interview, Irene the manager responsible for the recruitment decision carefully weighed Dylan's experience credentials against the job description and the other applicants. After she completed her round of interviews, it was clear that the other five candidates had Dylan well and truly covered for experience.

Once Irene had made her decision, Dylan was the first person she rang. Irene advised him that she would be taking a risk in employing him, given his limited background working in a challenging field. However, Dylan had convinced her that he was willing to deal with and turn challenge into opportunity. This included rattling traditional organizational cultures that often-sought command and control over their stakeholder and client relationships at the expense of respecting choice.

Given her years of experience and being a mother of two children with disabilities, Irene understood what type of person was needed for this role. Therefore, she chose to go with her instincts and select Dylan based on his character, inspiration, and because he had convinced her that this was not just a job but a mission he was pursuing.

This woman understood that while job descriptions have their place in recruitment selection, they don't always capture certain intangibles. She clearly saw him as someone with a bigger life's purpose driving his career. She saw in Dylan a commitment to ensure that the voices of the disabled are heard and their human needs are satisfied in a world that mainly looks down on them and shunts them to the side because of behaviors considered socially embarrassing.

True to his word, Dylan always acknowledges my brother's presence during our phone conversations, something that would not be considered a key performance indicator in a call centre job. However, for someone with a disability who wants to be treated as an equal and to have his voice acknowledged, it is a precious gesture, influencing my brother's self-esteem. Dylan lives and breathes the message that my brother's life is important.

The Coronavirus epidemic that hit the world in early 2020 will be remembered as one of the greatest challenges faced by the world outside wartime. It has been a period that has seen countless lives lost, massive economic turbulence, higher unemployment, and a disruption to daily life.

It's a testament to Dylan's character that he created a career opportunity at a time of chaos when millions of people lost their jobs. I have shared his story because it is rare to find a person in their mid-twenties that has connected their career with a life's purpose. That is one of the major pillars that supports my definition of the Career Success Code. This is something I, personally, did not wake up to and act on until the middle years of my life. Many others, unfortunately, never connect with theirs or if they do lack the courage to travel that path.

While Dylan's starting point, career ideals, and destination will be different to yours, when a career comes to a turning point and a change in direction is needed, his story provides valuable guidance into a truly successful career. During my conversations with Dylan, I was able to put the pieces of the puzzle together which I share below.

Dylan's Career Success Code

1. **Taking the Lead** – Dylan did not sit idly by and tolerate an unsatisfying situation or simply wait for a better future

to arrive on his lap. He took the bold action of leaving the old and stepping into the new.

2. **Responsibility Clarity** – Dylan understood that subordinating to his manager for his work responsibilities did not apply when making career decisions and controlling his destiny.

3. **Embracing Challenges and Turning them into Opportunities** – Dylan recognizes that leaving the call centre did not eliminate challenges, it simply created different ones. The type of challenges he now deals with energize rather drain him because he can see the opportunity they create. The traditional bureaucratic organizations he interacts with provide him with the opportunity to further develop his creative entrepreneurial core skills and potentially elevate his career to the next level by inventing a new model that renders the existing obsolete.

4. **Pleasure in the Work** – Dylan clearly enjoys working with the disabled. His enthusiasm and vitality are qualities rarely seen in many workers. The pleasure he experiences when he sees the smile on a client's face because they have overcome a fear, learnt a computer skill or added to their vocabulary may be taken for granted by most people, but represent tiny miracles for Dylan.

5. **Mission with a Message** – Each time I speak with Dylan it becomes clear that he is someone on a mission with a clear message that frames his decisions and actions. Like his boyhood hero – his message drives a sense of urgency, an unrelenting can-do attitude and a single-minded focus on moving organizational cultures to a new way of thinking. Thinking that recognizes that a shift in power is needed away from command and control minded disability providers to choice and control to the person.

6. **True to your Nature** – When you interact with Dylan you know you are dealing with the true person. Many

people put on a façade, speak in a formal voice and dress differently to play a role. As the late Jim Morrison lead singer for the rock band, "The Doors" once said, "most important freedom is to be what you really are".

Whether discussing business or personal matters, it's the same Dylan you interact with – who he is and who you get. There is no identity crisis coming his way anytime soon.

7. **The Wisdom of Mentors** – The memory of a life cut short at 18 is a constant reminder for Dylan that time is precious and that we don't have the luxury to make every mistake in the book. This provides him with the incentive to draw on the wisdom and experiences of mentors who provide him with different perspectives on his challenges, allow him to bounce ideas and give him a glimpse of a potential future that may be beyond his vision today.

As his main work mentor shared with me, who by the way is also the wise person instrumental in his recruitment – "Dylan has gone from my may be later interview basket to my star performer".

Dylan's career code goes beyond achieving the usual outer measures of success, such as money, material symbols, and power. Unlike most people, Dylan's career is inspired by a yearning inside him that comes from his personal journey. His experiences instilled a sense of family, the loss of cousin Robbie, and the need to fulfill a cause based on what he perceived as missing. Namely, the unheard voices of those less-able but whose message needed to be expressed and heard.

An experience that affirms Dylan's definition of career success happened as I was completing this chapter. I share it here because it demonstrates the difference between a day job and a career that nourishes a heart and satisfies a life.

I rang him first thing on a Monday morning for a status update on one of my brother's planned service requirements. When he answered my call, I was greeted by a person who sounded like he had the life taken out of him—a far cry from the high-energy and enthu-siastic tone of voice that usually greeted me.

Dylan explained that he was at a veterinary clinic because his six-year-old grey cat Pierre was about to undergo surgery. His life hung in the balance because of kidney stones that were blocking his urinary system. During the week, I rang a few times to check on Pierre's well-being and how Dylan was coping.

As the week progressed, Dylan's spirit slowly lifted, but it was not because of an improvement in Pierre's condition. The outpouring of love and support from his family of work mates and clients that took an interest in both him and Pierre had touched him deeply. They were seeing him through a painfully emotional life experience.

Many only belatedly discover that it's not just the external symbols that represent career success, it's also the internal ones. Being uplifted and supported during a time of need by a lot of human caring may well and truly override the external.

In case you are wondering whether Pierre is still with us, the answer is yes. Maybe Pierre has also been helped by the love of a bigger family that surrounds him that Dylan's career path has made possible.

You can reach Tony at tonypisanelli.com/

7

WEALTH CO-CREATION

CLIFFORD TODD

Imagine you're at a party, or anywhere small groups gather for conversations. You wander from group to group, listening for a clue for a conversation to join.

Do words about wealth or creating wealth intrigue you?

This chapter talks about three essentials to creating wealth:

- Something you enjoy doing that generates income
- People willing to help your efforts
- Minimizing the taxes you pay

What you enjoy doing is your vehicle to wealth. **Enjoying is essential.** Wealth normally builds up over time, so do something you enjoy doing well enough to create a sustainable base for wealth buildup. As a vehicle, what you do (or plan to do) can be fast, slow, or somewhere in between. Steven Covey taught *"Start with the End in Mind."* Choose your vehicle to wealth.

No one creates wealth all by oneself. Quantum physics says we live in one universe, connected as one energy field. The simplest plan to achieve wealth and success is to surround yourself with people who will work with you.

They are an essential component.

What you keep is more essential than what you earn. While this sounds obvious, it's rarely observed. Start with a tax-saving strategy.

I use the above bullets to present these ideas. These bullet points are simultaneous: you need a **vehicle, people,** and a **tax-saving strategy**, preferably all three at the get-go.

We all want more love in our lives. Our hearts never lie to us.

Creating wealth takes courage. I'm past halfway to 150 years old. I live my values and beliefs.

Three sets of people embrace this work: (1) companies that first care for employees to maximize profits, (2) non-profit organizations whose lifeblood flows through memberships and donations, and (3) health care practitioners. What's fascinating is how diverse groups embrace the same vehicle to serve their people. They all offer wealth and better health, both of which are essential to enjoying life.

I practice love and service. I teach love and service. I help people:

- Save money
- Enjoy positive cash flow
- Develop wealth-creating income
- Improve health, in a few hours per week, in sequential moments based in love, all within six to nine months.

My vehicle is **Wealth Co-Creation**. I worked full-time in medicine and side-timed network marketing. I had a few successes. My best ninety-day effort generated a $26.118 check; my best single check was $62,234. Most of the time I felt like a hamster on a wheel, spinning, getting nowhere.

In 2016, *in one day* I released a forty-year habit of drinking a bottle of wine every day. Inspired, I vowed to help people who try network marketing businesses succeed. It's grossly wrong that a single network marketing superstar earns more than the nine who earn some income combined with the 990 who try and quit.

Cancer derailed this effort. By 2019, I recovered enough that the U.S. Office of Patents and Trademarks registered my key network marketing training program, the **Moment Time**® conversational sequence. The Great American Writing Contest awarded me a $25,000 non-cash mentoring Grand Prize to write **Wealth Co-Creation**.

Applying **Wealth Co-Creation** takes the courage to be a home-based business owner (you can simultaneously be an employee or own another business) and the willingness to let go of negative biases against network marketing. Simply, you need to embrace a supportive mindset. Got it? Great! You can now co-create your wealth.

Wealth Co-Creation happens in four easy, *near-simultaneous* steps:

- Implement up-to-date tax-saving strategies as a home-based business owner, saving you thousands of dollars every year and generating positive cash flow from the get-go.
- Implement quantum physics energy medicine technology, even if you don't know how it works.
- Build your network marketing team using the *Moment Time*® people connecting skills, where 92% of your moments are focused on building loving relationships.
- Implement a tracking system and monitor your progress.

You will experience more **love, happiness, and joy** in your life as you **fund your dreams.**

Tax Strategies

We recommend you use five strategies to convert your personal expenses into business tax deductions.

1. Designate a visually discrete part of where you live. I live simply and work on two tables pushed together in the dining area of a one-bedroom apartment.

2. Put your car key in the ignition. Drive relaxed, knowing Uncle Sam is paying for the gas. Plus!

3. Pay your kids to work in your business. Family keeps the money; kids pay no taxes.

4. Never eat in a restaurant alone. Never vacation again. Meals and even family travel are business trips.

5. Establish a Health Reimbursement Plan. Deduct all of your family's health and wellness expenses.

Implement these expense conversions, and **join the most tax-advantaged taxpayers** in America! The sixth tax **WOW** is zero tax on 20% of net business income. My tax mentor expert is Ron Mueller, MBA, Ph.D.

Quantum Physics Energy Medicine

Quantum physics may be new to you. It's the study of energy and matter. 2,000 years ago, a goldsmith brought a lightweight plate to Tiberius, emperor of the Roman Empire. When asked how he made it, the goldsmith explained he had done so from common clay, by a process known only to himself and the gods. Tiberius feared that if people had access to this cheap metal, his gold would lose value. He beheaded the goldsmith. Civilization lost access to aluminum for 2,000 years. And yes, this is the Roman emperor that ordered Jesus to be crucified.

Our culture reveres science. We use quantum physics energy medicine. The company's cloud technology transmits the most relevant nutritional essences based on our individual energy patterns twelve times per day. When you implement this energy medicine, you'll be healthier, more productive, have fewer sick days, and incur less degenerative conditions. Subscriptions for this service drive **Wealth Co-Creation.** (Company policy restricts my using its name in personal literature. I'll let you know when we connect.)

Build Your Team

Moment Time® is the patented and registered conversational sequence we use to build network marketing teams. Its six love-infused steps are:

1. Friending
2. Clarifying
3. Trusting
4. Inviting
5. Joint Deciding
6. Player Coaching

Friending. Imagine you are four years old. Your mom takes you to a playground. Do you want to meet a new kid to play with? Same idea here, except now your mirror neuron radar picks a heart-savvy person before words are ever spoken. Consider this Og Mandino quote:

"And how will I confront each whom I meet? In only one way. In silence, and to myself, I will address him or her and say, "I Love You." Though spoken in silence, these words will shine in my eyes, unwrinkle my brow, bring a smile to my lips, and echo in my voice, and his heart will be opened."

Mirror neurons mutually fire when you act and when another's eyes observe your action—and they react the same way. You know who is loving you without saying a word. Hang out where people relax for a short time. I like coffee shops. Invest fifteen minutes getting to know someone your love radar identifies for you.

Note: Moment Time® is a patented registered sequence of moments. Ask yourself in every moment if you want to meet this person again. If yes, ask the other person to meet again, and if mutually yes, set the time and place. Every two weeks, start twelve people into *Friending*. As a guideline, ask six of those people into *Clarifying*, four of those six into *Trusting*, and invite two of the four into *Jointly*

Deciding. On average, one person every two weeks will join your team.

Clarifying. People love to talk about themselves. During this thirty-minute moment, ask the person what lights up her or his life. Keep the person talking with a simple, "tell me more about that," or, "if you had that, what would that do for your family or community?" Just listen. Do not advise or fix anyone. How long has it been since anyone just listened to you? It's rare, isn't it? Did you feel understood? Cared for? If yes, you experienced *Agape* love in action. Proceed as noted.

Trusting. During this forty-five-minute moment, listen to your new friend as a venture capitalist would listen to a person presenting their business plan. Stay accepting and loving. Offer ideas. Do not criticize or try to fix the plan. The goal is to build mutual trust. Proceed as noted. (Conversational guidelines offered on request.)

Inviting. This is a thirty-second step. Ask. "Would you like to talk about how some of my friends and I solve challenges and achieve dreams similar to yours?" Ask, then **shut up** and wait for an answer. Proceed as noted.

Jointly Deciding. Invite your Player Coach (enroller) to join you in this three-way conversation. Share your ideas about this business and how it works. Ask for your guest's feedback. You are in control. If you don't feel it's a mutual fit, don't ask the person to join you. If it's in both your best interests, cue the Player Coach to ask the joining question. If the answer is yes, your new heart-centered, business-savvy friend joins your team. If the answer is no, your guest says no to your Player Coach. Your friendship stays loving and secure.

Player Coaching. Continue loving and nurturing your relationships with your teammates and help them grow their teams in their *Jointly Deciding* moments. When you join my team at whatever level, I (or my team member) am your Player Coach. We, together, teach you the complete system.

Note: Moment Time® strips twentieth century networking of its flaws. **No selling:** the twenty-first century business model relies on people checking out products and services on the internet before they buy. **No inventory:** it's personal subscriptions. **No recruiting:** people agree to listen to how you and your friends achieve similar goals. **No personal rejection:** guests say yes to you, no to your player coach. The new twenty-first century networking business model is **UNIQUE, POWERFUL, and LIFE-REINVENTING.**

TRACKING

How much income will it take to fund your dream lifestyle? How long are you willing to put in the effort to create income? When you use twenty-first century networking, you will achieve your dreams faster than most people ever imagine.

For fifty years, superstars hid the truth. No one earns big paychecks from scratch. Imagine you are a pro-football halfback. Ball on your goal line. **Reality:** getting to your one-yard line takes two to three months. Building your team to reach the ten-yard line takes another two to three months. During the third set of two to three months, you rocket ninety yards and score (a six-figure annual residual income). When you use **Moment Time®**, you waste no time working with the wrong people.

My soon-to-be-released book, *Fun, Easy, and Profitable,* has charts of team size and income realized when quantum physics energy medicine subscriptions drive sales. *Under ideal growth, you will earn a five-figure monthly income in less than six months.* Few teams grow this fast. Your team is dynamically growing. If your team grows slower, keep going. You enjoy continual positive income. Your residual income will grow soon enough to fund your desired lifestyle. Relax. You will be free to do whatever you choose soon enough.

Three diverse sets of people endorse this work. Confidentiality keeps names confidential. Employers, non-profit organizations, and health care practitioners offer money and better healthcare to their communities. The key to these applications is how tax benefits keep the people's cash flowing positively, so no one goes net out of pocket. If you ever tried network marketing, you know how extraordinary not losing money is.

Time is easy. **Moment time**® takes six hours per week, and 92% of your moments are devoted to fun: building deep relationships. No painful days or hours are needed to build teams.

Finally, the incomes earned are life-reinventing **with no downsides.**

When you use **Moment Time**® and invest occasional moments tracking the personal spending you convert to business expenses, you will feel and be:

- **UNFORGETTABLE**
- **INFALLIBLE**
- **UNSTOPPABLE**

Call To Action

Weigh your rewards against the risk. What weighs more for you, the rewards or the risk? When new, loving relationships, enhanced health, and wealth outweigh paying a small subscription fee, please join us. You'll be glad you did.

You can reach Clifford 513-348-7872 and clifford@cliffordtodd.com.

He lives these words:

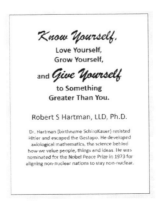

8

A 7-FIGURE BELIEF

ALINKA RUTKOWSKA

As I go through last month's revenue I can hardly believe it. My eyes seem to be popping out as I absorb the numbers. I used to dream of making one tenth of it. Now my wildest dreams have come true.

You will hear that wealth comes with sacrifices, that you never see your family and your health deteriorates. Oh, and that it's hard to make money, that's another one.

Here's the thing. While I'm in the 7-Figure range I only work four hours in the morning and two hours in the evening. I spend the rest of the time celebrating delightful Italian meals and playing with the kids on the beach.

I usually do a 36-hour email detox over the weekend.

So how did this all happen? I'm writing this both for you and for me because I need to wrap my head around it as well.

It started with a belief.

When I was a teen a book in the bookstore caught my attention. It was entitled "Think and Grow Rich". No-one had ever mentioned it to me before. I didn't know how celebrated the author, Napoleon Hill was.

The title was enough to convince me to devour the book.

I knew I could think.

And I believed that this book would show me how to think and grow rich.

Napoleon Hill taught me something else as well. Thanks to this experience I discovered that books can change lives. Twenty years later, as CEO of Leaders Press, I'm helping people write and launch books that change both the authors' and the readers' lives.

My first goal was to get a swimmer's certificate. I wasn't a great swimmer. "Think and Grow Rich" explained how to visualize your goals as having come true, so I visualized myself swimming and passing the test. I kept doing that for the upcoming months. I got that certificate.

That was proof enough for me that the system worked.

I kept setting goals for myself: winning the English contest, getting more certificates, getting into the best high school, getting into the best business school, finding a well-paid internship, getting a great first job.

I did all those things. When I was around 25 I told my then boyfriend and his mother that I want to be making $10k a month when I'm 30. They looked at me funny. His mother smiled mildly and nodded. They thought my head was in the clouds.

I then learnt to keep my revenue goals to myself.

I was a couple years late in achieving that $100k+ a year mark but I still got there. I had achieved my goals. Now what?

I started hanging out in circles where people were more successful than I was. It was natural for them to talk about $100k months. That stretched my thinking. I never had a $1M a year goal but I did some math, looked at my business and decided that I could pull it off.

I believed I could.

Of course I didn't have everything figured out.

While I got to the $100k month pretty much on my own (with one or two part time VAs), I got to $1M with a team. They deserve to be mentioned in this book as much as I do, so I want to thank my closest team members for believing in my vision and working towards it with the same passion I do.

We made a lot of mistakes. But then again, how else could we have learnt? Each business is different and you can't take anything for granted. I've invested in advertising that was a big money suck and never brought any ROI. I chased shiny new objects. I tried to latch on to anything that would increase our results.

But I also made a few good decisions. The best ones were to join and actively participate in masterminds. And then to immediately implement what I've learnt.

"Who seeks, finds".

So simple, yet so true.

You need to ask questions. And you need to be mindful of who you're asking.

If you want to make a million dollars, you need to ask a million-aire how to do that. But not a millionaire who inherited or married into money (which I think is awesome but not relevant to your question). You need to ask a self-made millionaire.

But not any self-made millionaire. You need to ask a millionaire who made their money through activities that you want to pursue (roughly).

So if you're thinking about an online business, pick the brain of a successful online entrepreneur, because that's quite different from an offline business.

Try getting into masterminds where people are at a higher level than you are. You know what they say, if you're the smartest person in the room, you're in the wrong room. Leave right now because you're not growing.

Test, implement and believe.

There are many traits successful entrepreneurs have in common but there's no cut and paste recipe for success.

There is a hack though :)

Do you want to hear it?

Scenario A: Your current morning.

If you're like most people, you turn on your phone as soon as you wake up. You check your email right away. What you see in the mail determines your mood. If it's good news, you're pumped up, if it's bad news you get up with a sigh.

You are giving other people (those who sent you emails) the power to dictate your mood - first thing in the morning - and that sets the tone for the day.

You probably check the news, because you need to be informed. The news however is not meant to inform. It's meant to shock. So you get shocked, then you get caffeinated because you need energy to start the day.

While you're sipping your coffee you're scrolling your social media feeds getting bombarded by other people's feelings and opinions that influence your mood even further.

Sounds familiar?

Scenario B: My current morning (this can be your morning starting tomorrow).

I wake up an hour before I need to wake up my kids. The alarm clock on my phone says "Wakey, wakey. All my dreams come true". I read it and I smile. I feel blessed to be waking up and hearing the sound of the waves crashing on the shore. I look at my little munchkins who are still asleep. I smile and realize I've always dreamt of this and it came true. A house by the sea, a phenomenal husband, two wonderful children, a thriving business.

I get up, do the human stuff and drink a glass of water with lemon. I look at the sea and the green hills surrounding the bay and feel blessed to be living in this magnificent setting.

I take my computer to the garden and turn on a 7-minute video of Qi-Gong. If you haven't heard of it you're in the minority. It's the #1 most widely practiced sport in the world. I sit down and meditate for a couple of minutes. Nothing fancy, some deep breaths, head movements and I list 10 things I'm grateful for. I watch my mind movie (mindmovies.com), which shows images and videos of my dreams with affirmations and inspirational music.

Then I go back inside, turn on my phone but only to listen to some opera while I prepare breakfast. I haven't checked my email once.

I get the kids ready and when I sit in front of my computer 90 minutes after I wake up I start with the mind movie again (it's only 2 minutes long).

I then look at my calendar and plan the four hours I have available today.

I always start by checking my finances and company scorecard. I check if we're hitting this week's target and what we need to do to hit it or exceed it.

I follow up on the items that will allow me to hit the targets. That usually takes an hour. I then have 3 hours left. I usually don't have any meetings in the morning (I'm in Europe and work mostly with the US).

I block the last hour of the morning for email. That leaves me with two hours.

I usually spend 30 minutes on email marketing. That leaves me with 90 minutes. I usually spend 30 minutes on strategy and 60 minutes on operations, mostly delegating stuff to the right team members.

At 1:00 pm I'm done and I won't check my email until the evening when I'm busy speaking to clients, prospects and partners for two hours every evening.

Do you see the difference?

Everybody has a different routine and while mine works for me perfectly, you might want to mix things up or eliminate some items. Maybe you want to go for a 60-min jog? Do it. I can't because I can't leave my kids home alone! Your routine will be tailored to your lifestyle just like mine is, but make sure you have one.

If you act on only one thing from this chapter, act on this: turn on your phone 30 minutes later than usual and do something uplifting instead of scrolling through social media feeds. My whole morning routine is uplifting but you can also choose to watch an inspirational video instead (or on top of it).

I don't know if this chapter alone will drastically change your life but I do know this: if you can believe you can make your dreams come true and you keep asking questions and implementing, you will.

Just like I did with Leaders Press where I'm blessed to be helping entrepreneurs turn their book ideas into best-sellers.

You can reach Alinka at Leaders Press.

9

CREATE A BUSINESS THAT IS TRUE TO YOU

KAREN FERREIRA

I'd been milling this over for a few weeks. One day, while walking the dog with my husband (and business partner), I came to a decision.

I told him, "You know, I've been thinking a lot. I've realized the whole direction we've been taking with our sales and marketing is wrong. We're trying to be something we're not. We're trying to force it. That's why it's not working. I've decided to totally change our approach. We're not going to do this stuff we hate for one more day."

As I explained my thinking, he lit up by degrees. Soon, we were both excitedly sharing how unhappy we were with the way we were doing things. It was a considerable relief that I'd realized this and that we could change it.

At that point, I knew I'd spotted something life-changing, but I didn't quite realize to what extent it would change things.

We had been working on the business for a few years, listening to plenty of experts and trying numerous ways to generate leads and sales. Still, it remained a day-to-day, week-to-week, month-to-month battle. It was just never what we envisioned when we spoke about our dreams for the business and our lives. Often when we started something new, we were so excited and "knew" this would change everything for us forever...until it didn't.

We're both hard-working (you know, those consistent seventy- to eighty-hour weeks). We try to solve situations ourselves and avoid making excuses. We'll do whatever it takes to make it work. We're persistent to a fault. Ironically, that was predominantly our problem.

Instead of admitting something wasn't working, we'd keep going and going...and going.

Now, you do have to persist on a given course to get results. Very few, if any, paths you choose will get overnight results. But by "it wasn't working," I don't mean we weren't getting results. I mean it was making us miserable.

I believe that to succeed you have to step out of your comfort zone sometimes, but that's markedly different to doing something you hate every day with dogged persistence because you think, "This is *the* solution that will make our business work." Even if it works (and thus you keep doing it), it may give you a successful business, but is that the life you want?

So, after loads of persisting on avenues I hated, and doing plenty of soul-searching, I realized you have to learn to discern between fear or discomfort versus that which goes against your grain, against your inherent personality.

Being fearful doesn't mean you shouldn't do it, but feeling it's wrong, painful, unethical, or absolutely not who you are, probably *does* mean you shouldn't do it.

I had the two confused. When a task felt agonizing and I knew I'd never enjoy doing it and it wouldn't fulfill me, I thought I just felt that way because I was fearful of doing it. That it was simply outside my comfort zone.

When I realized that was bullcrap, I had the epiphany I needed to build a business that suits who I am. That's when my business—and life—started changing.

The irony is that I was doubting and pushing myself, even though I knew I often did things outside my comfort zone. I'm persistent and driven, and when I put my mind to something there ain't no mountain high enough to keep me from achieving it. You might be the same, but don't let that lead you to persisting on the wrong path.

Something that resonates with who you are may still scare you, but it will also feel right or exciting on some level.

Okay, I realize I've been fairly general so far, so let me get more specific. First, let's consider why you'd let yourself get convinced to walk down a path you hate.

Well, if you're reading this book, I can bet you've been to a webinar, or something similar, where the host explained a problem to which you responded, "Yes, that's me! I want to solve that!" Then they presented a solution, but they presented it as *the* solution. The *only* solution. Without this thing, you'd never solve your problem. You know what I'm talking about, right?

Some people are fantastic at selling. They sell their solution really well. I'm not saying these are poor solutions or tools. Some of them are superb. But *none* of them are the *only* solution.

Need to generate traffic? There are many ways to do so.

Need leads? Again, there are a multitude of ways.

Sales, marketing, how to deliver your services, on and on—each one has two, or five, or ninety ways that you could achieve your goals.

Certain methods are better than others, sure, but the question isn't, "Is it better?" **The question is, "Is it better for *me*?"**

Okay, that brings me back to persisting down yonder chosen path against all internal resistance. Why would you do that? Well, because you believe there's no other path to success. Plus, you don't know yourself well enough—or you're not honest enough with yourself— to realize this is not the solution for you.

To be clear, I think almost all jobs will have parts you may not enjoy, that don't excite you. Like financial admin. Yuck. But that's not what I'm referring to; I'm talking about the stuff that makes your skin crawl.

Like, for me, an example of this is jumping up and down and shouting about how my product is the best product out there and how nothing else can do what it does at all, and if you don't get my product, and only my product, you are doomed to failure. Okay, maybe that's harsh, but some very successful people sell like that and they seem totally okay with it. I'm not.

A less extreme example is something as simple as cold calling. There are people who don't mind cold calling. I, for one, know a few people who enjoy it, and they've built amazing businesses using cold calling as a major part of their successful strategy.

For me, cold calling is more or less on a par with a gruesome medieval torture method.

So, is cold calling a good or bad business strategy? The answer is, it's neither. It's good for some, and bad for others.

This may sound so basic that you might be thinking, "Everyone knows that." Maybe, but this fact is easy to lose sight of in our day-to-day lives, when you're trying so hard to succeed. You lose track of yourself, you lose track of what resonates with you. And then, even if you "succeed," you'd only have created a monster that you have to keep feeding every day.

If (or as soon as) you can afford it, you can outsource the tasks you hate. But when we start out, we're more or less doing it all ourselves. So, create a business that is true to you.

For me, that meant no longer forcing myself to chat to strangers on LinkedIn, finding something to be interested in about them (which is actually easy for me), then chatting about that, but all the while knowing the purpose is to somehow steer them to a sale. I can't tell you how much I hated that approach.

My solution included taking all my focus off the money. Money has never been a driving force for me, and as long as I kept focus on it (because business is about making money, right?), I struggled, not only to make money, but also to enjoy myself.

One email from a person saying how much I helped them makes me smile much more than five thousand dollars landing in my account, even if I'm having a lean month.

My solution meant I stopped trying to sell. I stopped making videos where I tried to imitate an excited "someone-who-is-not-me" to convince others how amazing my product or service was.

It meant I stopped forcing myself to create content that felt meaningless and which I had no interest in sharing.

Yes, it can take a lot of searching to discover the right solutions for you. If you know how many books and articles I read, courses I did, videos I watched, and other training I pursued, you might laugh (or cry). I persevered because I knew there must be answers out there.

What I overlooked was that I had to determine they were the right answers for *me*. Keep that in mind from the start (or from today), and it will save you a lot of time, heartache, and money!

That's why I'm not writing this chapter about specific tools or approaches. The whole point is that what worked for me may not work for you. Methods that rocketed some people to success didn't work for me.

One thing that did work for me is virtual summits. Investing in Navid Moazzez's Virtual Summit Mastery was one of the best things I've ever done. This also raises an important point: it definitely scared me to approach and invite influencers to speak at our summit. *Then* I had to interview each person—on video—for other people to watch! I was *so* nervous!

But fear, or being out of my comfort zone, is not the same as a course of action feeling *wrong*.

It never felt wrong. I didn't feel I was going against who I am. Sure, there were moments when I thought, "Who am I to do this?" but I knew I was creating something valuable for my audience. I have a passion for it. The more interviews I did, the more I enjoyed it, and the audience loved it.

That's where my business changed. We grew a list of people who enthusiastically support what we do. Now I get to share stuff with them that I'm excited about, and I don't have to sell it. I can just share it with genuine excitement, and the rest follows naturally.

I worked on creating my newest courses full-time for weeks. Only once they were complete and we had to set up the sales pages did I think about money for the first time. I had effectively forgotten I was making them to sell. I simply made them for those who had asked for this know-how. For those people who had emailed me in the past about my other training and thanked me, or told me how much it helped them. I just created the courses for them and enjoyed doing it.

When I realized I hadn't once thought about the money, I can't express to you the sense of fulfillment I felt. It comes down to having an approach that suits you, in a business that satisfies you.

Find which path and mentors you resonate with. I relate more with Ryan Levesque than Russell Brunson. Is one better than the other? No. They're just different. Just as you and I are different.

Find your correct path. I promise you, walking it will be so much easier than trying to climb a mountain each day against your own heart.

You can connect with Karen at GetYourBookIllustrations and Children's Book Mastery

10

SOMEDAY MAYBE - HARNESS YOUR TIME AND ENERGY

DANIEL LEE SMITH

The daily grind. After an hour in traffic I would arrive at 9 a.m., turn on the computer, then catch up with co-workers around the coffee machine. It was a slow start to the day, to say the least. From here it was a series of short sprints at the computer and in meetings, interspersed with more coffee and chats. This scenario is likely very familiar to anyone working in an office environment.

I think the waste of time was always known to me, but I didn't know how to change things up—and besides, that was just how it was. The spark for me was when I requested a change in work hours after starting a family. I was getting home late and time spent with my young children was not what I wanted it to be. I negotiated a 7:30 a.m. start with a 4:00 p.m. finish.....and my world changed.

For a start, because I was leaving early at the end of the day, I didn't get caught up in any extra time (emergencies, overruns, or even just not wanting to be the first one to leave). At the beginning of the day, I had a good hour and a half up my sleeve before the usual start, and productivity was up, up, up! With no distractions, I pumped out a good deal of my usual day's work before any general staff even hit the building. I then observed while people fluffed about for an hour or more before doing anything.

It hit me like a brick. Suddenly, this terribly inefficient system was staring me in the face. Wasted time, poor routines, low energy and terrible productivity. Worst of all, that time is stolen from other areas of people's lives—in my case, more hours with my family. This is how a great many (dare I say, virtually *all*) organisations the world over operate. I had taken one small step out, and there was no going back.

What if you could delete the daily commute? What if you could work when you were most productive? What if you were measured on your output, not your time at a desk? Or even just one of these? Let me tell you—not only would your productivity soar, your general well-being would increase, your time would free up, and you would have much greater choice on where you add value to the world. You could then define your success based on your own goals. You could invest more time into work/business, spend time with family, or travel to name a few.

Planning Step 1 - Now

The first step toward taking control of your time (or toward any change you might want to make) is to audit your current situation. What is working, what is not? What are the roadblocks? What resources or skills do you have available? There may be parts of your day that seem out of control in the current situation—for example, if you are an airline pilot, requesting to work from home is not an option for you. Or if you have young children, weekends and after school to bedtime are haphazard (we are not just looking at work hours. Examine your entire day). Don't be discouraged, put aside any objections, ideas or plans for later, and *only* explore the situation as it stands. Be thorough and very honest with yourself or the next steps will not address the real situation.

Planning Step 2 – Where?

If you could magically change everything right now, what would it look like? What is your dream day or week? Again, put aside any plans or objections and just think about what you want.

With that done, we need to take a few steps back. The dream day will likely seem so far out of reach as to be a fantasy. Forget all the stages between now and where you want to be. They will likely change a lot in the time it takes to achieve the goal. Focus on the first stage or two. What do these scenarios look like? Simply define what you want. As an example, in my case, the first step was to spend a little more time with my family, preferably at dinner time onwards.

Planning Step 3 – How?

Now that we have the Now and the Where (first steps only), we can join the dots with the How. This can take a bit of brainstorming, and often requires some out-of-the-box thinking. For that reason, I highly suggest running the question past other people once you have exhausted your ideas. Give them your Now and Where analysis and ask for their thoughts. Don't add in your thinking until after they give theirs. Then, mix it all up and see what pops out between you.

Sometimes the answers are obvious, but usually they are not. This causes people to give up, or to not even go down the planning path at all. Persevere.

The Missing Ingredient

If you perform the above planning steps strictly managing time, you will miss huge opportunities. There is another often overlooked element that modifies outcomes significantly: ENERGY.

In my opening story about changing my work hours, note that this did NOT decrease my required time in the office at all, nor the need to undertake a lengthy commute to work every day. It did, however, change three very important things:

1. Increased quiet time. Entering a quiet (virtually empty!)

office allowed for concentrated focus.

2. Breaking patterns. The new routine shifted me away from old routines and removed an element of peer pressure around how things are done. No more coffee chats in the morning (or at least not until I had churned out significant work), and no unnecessary working late.

3. Changed personal energy. A surprise to me was that I found my energy is high in the morning. I can get a LOT done compared to later in the day. Previously, I was wasting this time on low value activities.

The gains were excellent just taking the first two items into account. It was the third item that added the real benefit as it made the whole thing sustainable. My professional results were not maintained—they *increased*. This was on top of the primary goal of being home for dinner.

Consider your plan in the light of when you have high energy Which activities are best allocated to the various energy levels and are there activities that might feed or deplete your energy?

Action Time

With the hard job of figuring out what you really want and the even harder job of calculating the first couple steps both out of the way, it is finally time to make it happen. Even if you are a business owner or self-employed, this will likely require you to convince others and/or seek permission from somewhere.

Entire books have been written on the art of negotiation, but to give you a simple start, put yourself in their shoes. Try to make your request easy to say "yes" to. This means, at the very least, there is a neutral cost to them in giving it a go. Preferably, there are benefits. Set a trial period and do your utmost to make it work.

You will encounter the word "no" on this path. Always see this as "not now" instead of a straight "no." Just to name a few options, it might take a different pitch, better timing, or a different job to make this work. If applying for other jobs, give your honest reason for leaving your current employment—such as wanting to spend time with your children, or elderly parents, or whatever it is you want. If you get the job, you get your new conditions right off the bat. Many will respect those values, and if they do, you have found the right workplace for you.

Planning Step 4 – Periodic Review

Things change, and your steps or even the end goal might alter significantly over time. This is why we don't plan out more than the next few steps. You change jobs by choice or otherwise, you miss a deadline/goal, an opportunity emerges, a global pandemic makes everyone work at home! Go with it, and update your plan. You are not stuck with your first draft. When I look back at my path, I couldn't have planned it all at the start, but the desire for more control over my time was persistent, allowing opportunities to be recognised and acted upon.

One Journey

Flexible Hours —> Work from home —> part-time work —> self-employed —> *Business* —> *Give back (not retired!)*

Getting from step 1 to 4 (now) took five years, and in the process my income has *tripled*. I now work chiefly from home (that saves over 2.5 hours of driving each day), do the school runs most days as well as attend school events regularly. I spend time with my parents including a monthly lunch, something I couldn't do when working in the city. Flexibility at this time in life is priceless to me. A number of factors were involved, but the ability to control my time and energy is at the absolute core of where I am right now.

Managing your time and energy produces margin in your life. Margin gives you time to think, time for unexpected events, and time to spend with people who matter the most. Get that promotion, build that business, go to lunch with your parents, have breakfast with a friend, beat that last Xbox level. Most importantly, take time to think deeply. These things revive you and increase professional performance, not the opposite.

One last tip—learn from others but don't compare yourself to them. We are all dealt different cards and have different goals. The permutations and the definitions of success are endless. Run your own race.

Connect with Daniel at www.danielsmith.me

11

UNIQUE IDEAS HAVE THE POWER TO CHANGE THE WORLD

MARIE INCONTRERA

Let me paint a picture. I'm an artist, after all.

I'd recently turned thirty and was officially a decade into my career as an avant-garde musician. My career, as far as young, avant-garde careers go, was in a good place. Mine was the kind of career that brought me around the world, afforded me my own ensemble, and had me playing at places like Carnegie Hall. (In fact, my band's last performance was at Carnegie Hall—a concert that I'd largely bootstrapped. But that's a story for a different time.)

So when I got *the* text message—the one that would effectively change my entire life—I'd love to be able to tell you that I was backstage before a big performance, or holed up in a practice room working on my magnum opus. But the reality is far less glamorous.

I was in the middle of a particularly difficult odd job. I was the queen of odd jobs throughout my twenties—teaching music for cash, transcribing handwritten scores into notation software for master composers, gigging, administrative assisting, temping, the list goes on. I worked constantly and exhaustively, because the thing that they don't tell you in music school is that many musicians, no matter how successful, can never afford to retire. In fact, you can be good enough to put on a concert featuring just you and your band to a well-attended audience at Carnegie Hall, and still be broke.

And I was broke.

I was every cliche in the book: writing music into the night because I had no time during the day due to aforementioned odd jobs; eating cost-effective-yet-questionable food from packages (or, and I cringe to admit this now: scarfing down two slices of pizza on the way to the subway station); dwelling in a studio so cheap it afforded me bragging rights, but so small there was no room for anything but my bed, a bookcase, and a piano (which was also so cheap it afforded me bragging rights...although it wouldn't hold its tuning for longer than a couple of weeks).

But I didn't mind, not really. Being a starving artist is a form of paying one's dues to their art. Poverty in service of creativity is regarded as noble. An older mentor of mine used to say, with an air of reverence: "When I was your age, I never knew where my next paycheck was coming from."

So there I was: barely thirty, at a miserable odd job, probably in the middle of a blood-sugar crash from all the pizza. This is when I got a text message.

"I have an idea for you. Quit your job."

And if your friend jumped off a bridge...

I know, I know.

How many people in your life would tell you to quit your job? Moreover, how many people could send a text like that and get you to actually listen?

The text, though, is from my good friend Dorie Clark, who is a successful consultant, business author, and entrepreneur. Dorie is the kind of person who's never short of brilliant ideas. I know this because she's had game-changing insights about my music career—the kind that put me directly on the path to Carnegie Hall. And so, I've grown to take her ideas seriously. This one has a good plan behind it.

"Brand yourself as a virtual assistant. Once you have a few clients lined up, give notice. You'll probably make as much money as you're making now, if not more, and you'll have more time and energy for your music."

Here's why that was an easy sell, and one of the hardest things for me to admit for all of the internet to see: I'd come home with under $15,000 the year before.

I set things up and then set a date: May 16, 2016, my thirty-and-a-half birthday, was the day I'd begin with my new clients.

My virtual assistant work grew slowly but steadily for the first six months or so. After a while, private clients started coming to me, and I filled out my income and my time by working with a few online firms. As my clients' faith in me grew and more clients began to come to me via referral, my place in the market began to unfold.

Almost exactly a year in, a referral client came in the form of an email introduction. The client had a TEDx idea that needed to be pitched, and he was looking for a virtual assistant to do it for him. I didn't know much about TEDx talks, except for what I'd seen online. *Don't you have to be famous to do a TEDx?* I thought. I asked Dorie as much.

"You can do this," she replied. "Just look on the TED website."

I finally told the client, "No guarantees, but I can pitch you."

We agreed to try it for a month. By the end of the month, he'd gotten accepted to not one, but two—one that he'd pitched before we'd started together, and one that I'd pitched.

Word spread and another client came my way, requesting my services for TEDx pitching.

"No guarantees," I said.

Before long, he was booked for two talks over the next few months. A third client came my way.

"No guarantees," I insisted.

She was accepted for one and got into the final round of consideration for many others.

I decided it was time to learn to walk my talk. I knew that I wanted to give at least one TEDx talk, and I knew that I wanted to be as creative as possible, for two reasons—because I am a creative person, and because I wanted to test my theory on what makes for a great TEDx talk. I tried a few creative exercises that I'd learned in music school and applied them to my talk ideation.

The three questions that were most effective are the three questions that I ask all of my TEDx coaching clients in our first session, no matter where they are in the process:

1. What would you do for free?
2. What, if allowed, could you not shut up about?
3. What do people ask you to pick your brain about?

By asking myself these three questions, I had a list of things that meant a lot to me. Music, business, exercise (at the time, I was playing roller derby), innovation, scaling my business. I began looking for the threads between these disparate ideas, and found that there were a few interesting topics that weren't covered on the TEDx YouTube channel: Jazz as a model for business innovation, and exercise and earning potential. I crafted my pitches, and began to apply. And in August of 2018, I gave my two talks within less than two weeks.

My talks were an instant credibility marker. I became known as a TEDx expert, and I was able to solidify my TEDx offering. To date, I've helped dozens of clients get onto stages across the country and the world, and most of them have been accepted to more than one event. My signature framework helps people come up with ideas and talks that are unique. Not only do they become associated with the TEDx brand recognition, but they also give a talk that has not been given before.

Good ideas grab your attention, but unique ideas have the power to change the world. That's why the TED brand has endured - because Ideas Worth Spreading are powerful, global, and actionable things that take on a life of their own.

What I've outlined here for you is the Ideation process of my framework. To learn more about how to take your idea from the page to the stage, you can pick up a free copy of my book, *Spread Your Idea,* here: *http://bit.ly/freetedxbook*

The world needs your idea. So what are you waiting for?

You can reach Marie at incontrera.com.

12

YOUR HEALTH CODE

DR MARCUS CHACOS, CHIROPRACTOR

Success without health is not success at all.

In this chapter I am going to show you how you can have incredible health, energy, and vitality—and how to use this newfound state of being to create lasting and meaningful success in your business and in your life.

The *Success Code* discusses the pillars of success. I believe the pillar of health is pivotal if you are going to be successful. In this chapter, I'm going to discuss the 7 Pillars of Optimum Health—or what I call the Total Healing Blueprint—and how you can apply these pillars to create the life you desire.

Your body operates by universal laws. The body has, inherently, the capacity to heal. nWhen you function at a healed, peak level, your ability to succeed will be far greater. You will have greater energy, focus, and concentration. You will have increased drive and more episodes of insight and inspiration. You will be able to do and achieve more, because health is not just how you feel—it is how you think, act, and perform.

What you are about to learn are the principles I have used in my practice as a transformational chiropractor, delivering cutting-edge breakthroughs in the health and lives of my patients and the community. I've used these principles in my life to experience incredible health, energy, and vitality. They are the foundation for my success in practice and in life.

You can use this, too, to become a healthier, more successful you!

I believe the Total Healing Blueprint is the most powerful and transformative healthcare model—and the foundation for all success!

The reason this model is so powerful and profound is because it works on each of the 7 Pillars of Optimum Health, therefore building a platform for success. It is more than a health system; it is a model for personal transformation and peak performance living.

To give you an example, let me share with you the transformative story of Les. When Les came into our practice, he didn't walk in—he literally *crawled* in. He was booked in for surgery in six months' time. He was on the public system, so he had to wait for his surgery. He had a significant disc and arthritic injury and it was causing him unrelenting pain, impacting his mobility and his ability to function. He couldn't walk, he couldn't work—he couldn't do anything.

Let me show you what is possible. You might think it's a miracle, but it *is possible for everyone.*

Below is an example of what normal lower-back x-rays look like. You can see the normal shape of the bones of the spine and the dark space that the discs occupy between the vertebrae.

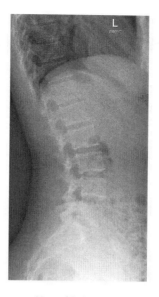

Normal Spine x-ray

The next image below is Les' x-ray. When we compare the two films, we can see that there is a severe loss of disc height as well as bone spurs and change of colour of the bone. This is indicating an advanced arthritic change.

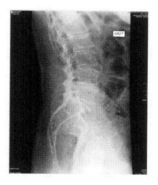

Les' 1st x-ray image

Finally, you can see Les's x-ray a year later, after noticeable healing has taken place. The discs are repairing, the bone spurs are lessening. Most importantly, he had no pain! In fact, he was pain-free after six weeks, and back at work not long after.

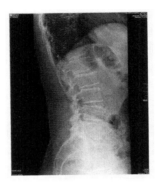

Les' 2nd x-ray image (one year later)

Not only that—he didn't require surgery, pain-killing medication, or anti-inflammatories. His body was able to function, perform, and do all the things that he wanted to do, including playing with his grandchildren, playing sports, and doing recreational hobbies on the weekend. It had a massive impact on his health and quality of life. He was able to succeed in his career and in his life.

This is massive. Pain limited his health, wealth, and success. This is why health is your greatest asset and the most important part of your personal *Success Code*. After applying the Total Healing Blueprint, Les could live his life fully and completely,

The key takeaway from this is that the body can heal. The body is designed to heal. Healing means peak performance living. Peak performance living means you will have greater energy, focus, and concentration. You will have increased drive and more episodes of insight and inspiration. You will be able to do and achieve more, because health is not just how you feel—it is how you think, act, and perform.

Health gives you the ability to achieve your goals and dreams.

That's where we come to the Total Healing Blueprint. If you apply each of the Seven Pillars of Optimum Health that constitute the Total

Healing Blueprint, the body has all of the resources it needs to heal and to function at peak levels of performance.

If you have a health problem such as arthritis, diabetes, or obesity (or even a genetic or lifestyle condition) and you feel like you can't make any change in this condition, that's a myth. The reason it's a myth is because most people don't apply each of the Seven Pillars of Optimum Health, so they are therefore not fully understanding the Total Healing Blueprint and the body's capacity to heal—in fact, totally heal and rise to its true potential.

The most common reason people fail to succeed in business or achieve their goals isn't a lack of knowledge, skill, or ability. It is their health, energy, and mental acuity that are lacking. *It is their health!*

The body was designed to self-heal, self-regulate, and self-organise. Equally, it was designed to thrive and function at heightened levels of performance.

Why doesn't this always happen?

The answer: because something has interfered with your innate intelligence, that inborn wisdom that governs and controls all functions within the body. When we identify what is interfering with this intelligence and we remove that interference, the body has the capacity to return to peak performance—peak performance healing, peak performance function, and peak performance living.

When free of interference, we not only function at our best—we experience insights, perceive truths, and have breakthroughs other people do not. You access a creative force when you are your best self. This is how your Total Body Health is both a competitive advantage in business and your *Success Code* for life.

Here are the potential areas of interference to the innate intelligence and those Seven Pillars of Health:

1. The nervous system
2. The physical body
3. The biochemical processes of the body
4. The emotional and mental states of being
5. The energetic systems of the body

6. The genetic influences within our body
7. The spiritual world

When we implement strategies across each of these seven pillars, we have a Total Healing Blueprint. We have the possibility of addressing all the causal issues and areas of interference within our own body and mind.

Let's look a little deeper.

Interference to the nervous system can be caused by physical trauma, chemical trauma, and emotional trauma. Removing interference is effectively done through therapeutic means, such as chiropractic adjustment; osteopathic manipulation; or even breathwork, meditation, and homoeopathy.

Physical body trauma can result from injuries, such as car accidents or falls, as well as repetitive trauma, including being seated at a desk for a prolonged period of time or lifting, bending, and carrying the wrong way. Removing interference is effectively done through therapeutic means, such as chiropractic adjustment; osteopathic manipulation or bodywork; as well as stretching, strengthening, and conditioning exercises.

Biochemical trauma can come from the chemicals in the food that we eat or the water we drink, the pollution in the air that we breathe, as well as chemicals in our environment. Changing your diet and undertaking a detoxification program helps remove interference.

The stressful thoughts we have and our challenging emotional experiences can result in stress and cause interference. Getting enough sleep; having enough rest and relaxation; as well as meditative practices and breathwork exercises assist in restoring the emotional and mental balance.

Energetic interference results from excessive exposure to artificial light, computer screens, mobile phones, and other technological devices. To remove this interference, unplug and spend more time in nature.

Spiritual interference occurs when you do not have clarity about your meaning and purpose in life; you do not have peace, love, and forgiveness in your heart; and you are not moving in the direction of your potential. To achieve this, apply meditation, prayer, visualisation, and other holistic spiritual practices I discuss in my Total Healing Blueprint training.

Your genetic blueprint can be either positively enhanced or destructively influenced by your lifestyle choices. The study of epigenetics shows that you *can* activate your healing potential and restore the body's natural state. It's not a question of *if*—but *how*.

What I found is that people are challenged with health concerns in today's society because most people live such a fast-paced, overwhelming lifestyle. They're not fully implementing and applying the principles that we've discussed here within the Total Healing Blueprint—but when they do, transformation is possible. And when I say transformation, that includes their health, their business, and the levels at which they succeed.

As this book discusses, there is a *Success Code*. There are things that you can do in order to achieve success. In my experience, the most successful people have the energy and vitality to do what they need to do, when they need to do it. Sustaining motivation, energy, and drive—all of this requires health.

In truth, the number one pillar of the *Success Code* is your health. As I've said earlier in this chapter, your health is your greatest asset— all of your other successes and financial assets depend upon it.

If you'd like to find out more about how you can experience incredible health, energy, and vitality; transform any of the health challenges you present with; and overcoming challenges to claim the success that you desire, go towww.totalhealingblueprint.com and I'll share *Health as a Success Code* with you. I will also provide solutions for you to overcome any health challenges you may be experiencing.

You can reach Dr. Marcus Chacos at totalhealingblueprint.com

13

YOUR "PLUS ONE"

FARHAN A. HAMIDANI

If there's one thing I can tell you about myself it's that I am addicted to Diet Coke. I drink a lot of it. I have reduced my intake now—I kind of had to as I got older—but five years ago, I was going through seven to ten cans a day, sometimes even more. I'm sure that made you cringe a bit. During my days of Diet Coke addiction, I had the opportunity to rent out a beautiful, luxury villa in Costa Rica where my family spent a week to celebrate our wedding anniversary. In addition to my wife and kids, I also asked my brother and brother-in-law to join, as we had more than enough space at this property.

The villa was incredible. It was a five-bedroom, five thousand-square foot property with a large, outdoor, private infinity pool overlooking the ocean. The greenery of Costa Rica was all around us; it was truly a magical place. When we first walked in, the property manager, Robert, showed us around and went over the basic details we needed to know to make sure the place worked exactly as we needed it to.

Then, as we were making our way back to the front of the villa, Robert put his hand on my shoulder and said, "Your travel agent also has a surprise for you." He grinned. I started wondering whether this whole property was a tease and a prank. I remember looking at my wife, giving her a defeated head nod. But, I went along with it.

"What's the surprise?" I asked, to which Robert began to give me light shoves to go into the kitchen.

"So what's the surprise?" I asked again.

Now he really got a sinister smile on his face. As he walked over, he yelled, "Open the fridge!"

I opened the fridge, and I kid you not, the smile on my face was bigger than seeing all of the features of this property combined. For me, even though I'd been to Costa Rica half a dozen times already, this had suddenly become the best vacation I ever had. The fridge was completely packed with Diet Coke. There must have been at least one hundred cans of it completely packed in there, maybe more. My agent had arranged to have this done in collaboration with the property manager, without me or my family knowing anything about it.

Think back to the last time you felt like that—isn't it just the best? You have this great feeling of joy, and it becomes ingrained in your memory as something you can never forget. Now, think about a time you did that for someone else. I'm not referring to just surprising someone, but instead, when was the last time you exceeded someone's expectations? And not just exceeded, but put things at a whole new level?

The Framework

In the mid '90s, I read a book called *Raving Fans,* authored by Ken Blanchard and Sheldon Bowles. The book was a huge success and is still one of my favorite books to recommend. The lessons outlined in this book continue even today, and are still lessons I give to new employees who join our organization.

Here is a key quote to summarize the main idea from *Raving Fans*:

"Your customers are only satisfied because their expectations are so low and because no one else is doing better. Just having satisfied customers isn't good enough anymore. If you really want a booming business, you have to create Raving Fans."

It's always been very important for me to always think of how I can create raving fans. It's become a fundamental minimum for me and my businesses. For me, it's the foundation upon which success is built.

If you look at the fundamental point of *Raving Fans*, the idea is that you provide your client or customer what they need or want, and then add something extra, a plus one, to exceed their expectations.

What a novel idea: exceed your client's expectations so they become raving fans of your business. Did my travel agent exceed my expectations? I believe he had already accomplished that by the property he had found for us. He blew past the "exceed expectations" marker by adding Diet Coke in the fridge. He also went one further and had a surprise birthday cake delivered to our villa as well. Now, I know that somewhere, somehow, I paid for all this, but I wasn't expecting it—at least, I didn't see it on my detailed itinerary.

I want to clarify, however: my definition of "Plus One" is a little different than Tom Peters' "Raving Fan" definition. In today's environment, meeting expectations is considered average. Look at any performance evaluation form, for example: "Meets Expectations" is right in the middle. It might as well just say "average" there. To be successful, you can no longer just meet expectations. The bar is currently at "exceeds expectations," and the "plus one" methodology is to add something extra after you have exceeded expectations. Meet, then exceed, and then plus one.

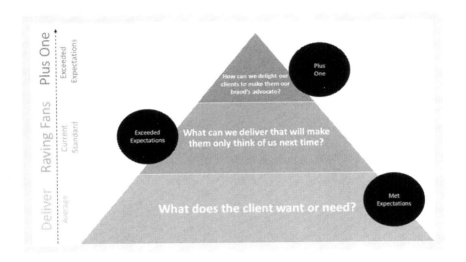

Application

Eleven years ago, when I was Senior Vice President at one of the largest independent financial advisory groups in Canada, I remember Dave, the CEO, saying to me that as a firm, we can't just provide operational services to the advisors who decide to partner with us as their licensing firm. We need to do more, much more. Otherwise, what's stopping them from going to another financial institution to manage their client assets there? How can we be different?

One of the main backgrounds in my career has been the training of financial advisors. Training in all areas, whether it's how they can run their business more effectively, portfolio management, or client servicing, and the list goes on.

To respond to Dave, I thought of an idea where we could develop an online program and make it one of the largest practice management platforms available for advisors to use. I remember saying to him that this would be huge.

"We can have content, tools, and resources for all key areas where advisors could use support," I said. "We don't necessarily need to reinvent the wheel, either. All of this content can be sourced from our various mutual fund company partners. We are simply organizing it, reviewing it, and putting it in a framework that they can utilize easily, or have their teams use."

Of course, my plus one on this was to provide training and education around using the tools, so that it was not just on a website. Instead, we were to actually show everyone how to use it. Of course, Dave did a plus one on top of that and hired someone to specifically work on a one-to-one basis with all our top advisors.

So there I went, starting to plan all of this out and thinking of a framework. Not only did the framework need to be relevant to the businesses the financial advisors were running, but I wanted to make sure they were delivering a *plus one* without even knowing it. The question I needed to answer was "how." How do I build it so our advisors were consistently trained to deliver "plus one" experiences?

Below is the framework we developed.

The important thing about this framework are the two ends—the beginning, which says "Prospect," and the end, which says "Advocate." The whole idea of this framework was to help an advisor take someone they don't know through their well-crafted processes so that this person, this prospect they don't know, at one point not only becomes a client, but also an advocate of their business. Basically, the client is now a walking, talking billboard of the advisor's practice and their services.

Now of course, the magic is in the last step: what are you going to do in the way you service your clients that not only exceeds, but provides that plus one service that goes beyond anything else that is being offered?

The plus one framework isn't only for services or products you sell. It applies at all levels in everything we do. I have always looked at anything I do from my client's point of view.

How do you define who your customer or client is? Isn't it the person who consumes the goods and services that I am selling/offering? Not exactly. If I'm an employee of a firm, yes, I can think the end product's clients are consuming from this organization. However, my immediate client, for me, is my manager. Or, since I manage my own businesses, I see my team and staff as important clients. You can't give your clients a plus one experience if your team hasn't experienced it themselves, and understand the framework and importance of it.

The Plus One Framework considers all stakeholders; it has to. It's not an option to make it applicable to one group over another. Using the framework sets the stage for your business's success, no matter how your clients interact with you or anyone else in your organization.

To illustrate the applicability of this framework in an employee/manager scenario, let's assume that I'm back in my corporate job at the bank. My boss tells me she wants to launch a new marketing strategy. She's very excited about it and, in her mind, she knows this will be an amazing, huge success. You may know that many leaders tend to have a number of ideas; it's up to their team to plan, develop, execute, and service these ideas. She goes on to suggest that it would be a good idea to have a strategy meeting with all the VPs and Directors to discuss this new plan and determine how we can make it happen. Let's break it down:

Her expectations: I go to her Executive Assistant and tell her to schedule a meeting, giving her the names of everyone who should be at this meeting.

Exceed expectations: I create an overview deck of the idea that outlines everything she told me. I put some discussion points in the document and have it circulated ahead of the meeting so everyone is up to speed and she won't have to repeat herself. We can now spend the meeting on actually planning it out.

Plus one: I do some research on whether the company has done anything like this before. I also research whether some of our competitors have launched this type of marketing scheme. I speak to some of the people who will be at this meeting and get some of their thoughts ahead of time to see where everyone stands. Then I draft a quick report for my boss to give her some background and give her an idea of some pros and cons. I even tell her which things people are liking about it, as well as some of the negatives people are thinking. This lets her get ahead of the situation and really lets her be in charge of the direction of the strategy session.

Yes, this may seem like a lot of work, but have I delivered a plus one? Sure I have. Will it be remembered? Yes, one hundred percent. This is a sure-fire way to make you an indispensable employee and ally with your boss. Do you have to do this every time? Absolutely not. You do it where you can. You don't do it often enough to change her expectations, but you do it enough that it's remembered.

However, there is a trap to the Plus One methodology. Since you become so used to providing plus one expectations, you have to be careful that your own expectations aren't raised. It's a common trap. If I'm providing plus one results to my boss, should I be expecting that from my team? Absolutely not, at least not until you have done your job in coaching them. Our jobs as leaders and managers is to support our employees and help them prepare for their next job. That's our Plus One to them. That's ensuring there is success at all levels.

You can connect with Farhan at www.tfglobal.com

14

HOW TO SUCCEED WITHOUT REALLY TRYING

ANGE HILSTRON

"Could do better if she tried harder!"

How did this simple remark on my school report affect my attitude to life?

I grew up during the Great Depression and at the beginning of World War Two, at age ten, I was evacuated to a rural school in Somerset. As the eldest girl in the country school, I was expected to tutor the younger children. After I finished my school work, I was sent outside to prepare the school garden for seeds, feed the chickens, and make notes about the weather.

Six months later, I was enrolled in a small private school in Surrey. My new private school was dedicated to bringing out the highest potential of its students. I was placed in a classroom with much older girls. Although academically it seemed a good idea, socially it was a mistake. I had nothing in common with the older girls. My school reports reflected my feelings of inadequacy and, far from being encouraged to do better, it seemed that the harder I forced myself to improve the more I failed. Instead of encouraging me to try harder it did the opposite and, paradoxically, I discovered the hidden secret to success.

By the time I was thirteen, the bombing of London was in full swing. I took my School Certificate examinations hiding in our school''s basement bomb shelter. My father left home to do war work and my mother took me out of school to look after my siblings while she went out to work. I wanted to go to an art college, but mother regarded art as a hobby and sent me to work in the city as a shorthand typist. I was hopeless at it.

However, I eventually secured a place at Wimbledon College of Art using a bursary I gained at the private school. I studied at night for five years and gained a Fine Arts Certificate that was beneficial toward a Bachelor of Arts degree later in life. I majored in cognitive aesthetic perception—in other words, why some people are aware of beauty and why others live in squalor. I was fascinated by human life-span cognitive development - how people learn skills throughout their lives.

I eventually became an Art Teacher after my husband and I, with a baby daughter, immigrated to New Zealand.

So how did I manage to succeed, having been constantly told that I needed to try harder? Watching my baby sister's efforts to crawl and then to walk made me realise that success happens naturally, whatever the circumstances. There was a critical time for learning each step. The process could not be forced. "Try" carried with it an implied expectation of failure. It assumed incompetence. No matter how hard one tried, unless the task was done properly, success may never be satisfactory. Learning the correct method was essential to a happy outcome.

The most successful thing a person ever did was to be born. Right from conception, the foetus grew in the womb in natural stages of development until it emerged as a personality. Considering the number of potential possibilities of failure when a sperm attempts to fertilise an egg, it was nothing short of a miracle that conception occurred at all. Given the right conditions, the offspring would flourish and succeed to adulthood without having to really try.

Success and competition often went together with the position of siblings within the family unit. I was the eldest, and therefore put in charge of my siblings. My brother was physically powerful, with a loud voice, while my baby sister had her own way most of the time. All forms of life compete with each other for survival. Plants compete for space and sunlight, animals compete for mates and territory. Humans compete for status. My road to success was in small steps, absorbing what I perceived as advantageous and not trying hard. I learned patience.

Planting seeds at the country school helped me realise that successful growth happened naturally, given the right conditions. It was necessary to prepare the soil for optimum results so the seeds germinated, put down healthy roots, and formed a good foundation for the plant to grow. I noticed that growth was not always upwards; it could be down as well as up, sideways, around, in and out. The beginning of a successful crop was in the preparation of the soil. So, in order to succeed, it was essential to do the groundwork, gathering as much information as possible. Preparation was tantamount to success.

As our family struggled during those early years with the loss of wealth and status brought on by the Great Depression, the outward trappings of success seemed less important than the perseverance to survive. I found that if I chose subjects and hobbies that I enjoyed, I tended to obtain better results. The key was not to seek fame and fortune, but do well in what I loved doing. Trying hard seemed to suggest tensing up and forcing a result, while letting it happen naturally meant relaxing and enjoying the journey. When those critical words were written on my private school report, I discovered the value of relaxed attention.

Because I opted out of the social stream at school, I spent a lot of time observing other people and exploring the natural world. At the rural school, I had been sent out to observe the clouds and the trees to determine what the weather was going to be that day. This was essential for a farming community. I made illustrated weather charts, beginning my love of painting and drawing. I discovered shared connections and interdependence with the natural world.

The American Dream supposed that anyone could become President of the United States of America. What was not explained was that a large capital was also a requirement. On becoming a successful person, a display of wealth was an important factor for maintaining success and status. Possessions, clothing, dwellings, business acumen, playmates, and friends in high places reinforced this value of esteem.

However, this cultural understanding was not shared globally. In some Pacific communities, fatness was considered a mark of success. In the Western world, thinness and an austere appearance denoted status. Displays of large estates and hugely decorated palaces described European values, while large armies and highly disciplined military power showed Asian societies as dominant.

This kind of display was not confined to humanity. Animals, birds, fish, and reptiles all decorated nests and displayed themselves to attract a mate. So, was success, with its wealth and gain of large territory, a means to attract an esteemed mate and ensure survival of the fittest?

"Judge your success by what you had to give up in order to get it." Dalai Lama, 2003.

In 1980, my husband reached the summit of his potential when he became CEO of a company. Our divorce enabled me to buy my own property and the opportunity to go to University to prove I was not as stupid as I appeared to be. My whole life expectancies changed, along with huge health challenges that required survival instincts lying dormant until now. Although I did not gain huge wealth or the trappings of wealth, I achieved great successes without trying very hard. It has meant certain sacrifices, but the journey has meant more to me than the destination.

The first step was not to take oneself too seriously. This was a game to be played with humour. Enjoy the process by choosing to be successful at things you love to do. Unless you are doing the tasks correctly, you will fail. Find out as much as you can about the subject to create a solid foundation. Research the market by watching and observing the world around you. Everyone is born with the potential for success; just being there is enough to affect others. Your responses and actions have a ripple effect on society's expectations of what is normal.

Your style of competitiveness may be the result of your position in a family unit. Competition occurs in all of life: everyone wants to be noticed, everyone wants to survive. The essentials for survival are water, food, shelter, comfort, clothing, and love. Growth may be stunted unless these needs are met. To be a success, you begin by providing these needs for yourself before you start to provide them for others.

In order to achieve success without really trying, you need to practice relaxed attention. Everyone has a different style for learning, but by releasing tension and remaining aware, much can be absorbed without trying. Virtual game players and fighter pilots practice the same technique - it can be an essential ingredient when everything is happening so fast it is hard to keep focused.

The aim is to achieve the best results for the least possible effort. Now is the best time to put these ideas into action, when the world as we know it is in chaos. The universe demands it!

Discover more Ange Hilstron books here:
> Any Excuse for a Party
> Rag Doll for Christmas

15

THE POWER OF THE PIVOT

PAUL BRODIE

My name is Paul Brodie. I am the CEO and book publisher of Brodie Consulting, a hybrid publishing and book launch marketing company. What we do is help medical professionals, attorneys, coaches, consultants, aspiring speakers, and business owners share their story by utilizing their book as the foundation of their business platform.

The theme of this chapter is about pivoting, and I want to share how I have pivoted multiple times over the past five years. Obviously, right now with what's going on in the world, a lot of people are pivoting. They're making changes. Many are changing their business model from a face-to-face model into an online business that they can grow locally, nationally and internationally. I wanted to share my story about this, because we have also pivoted multiple times.

Being a publisher was something I never thought was going to happen. My pivoting journey started in 2011. I was wrapping up my third year of teaching, and my health was a mess. I was roughly 340 pounds and my doctor told me if I didn't get my act together, I'd be dead in five years. So, I changed my habits and created a much healthier lifestyle. I was able to lose a significant amount of weight and keep it off. This inspired me to want to share my story.

My end goal was to become a motivational speaker and author because I wanted to share this testimony and help other people who were also struggling. However, what happened was that I had no idea how to write or publish a book, so that part got pushed to the sidelines for over four years. Finally, in 2015 I decided to finally write my book. I had an epiphany on a flight to Las Vegas where I decided to stop making excuses and get the book completed.

In Vegas, I created the outline of the book by the pool at the Mirage. A week later, over July 4th weekend, I wrote 20,000 words. That became the base of my first book.

Next, I had to figure out how to get this book published. I spent half the day learning everything possible about book publishing. Ironically enough, there was a virtual summit about book publishing that was going on at the time, so that helped a great deal. I spent the other half of the day doing research on the internet and learning everything possible about marketing, because I wanted my first book to be successful.

I was able to create the base and the foundation of our business by using what I learned. That wasn't the intention, but that's exactly what happened. A month later, we launched the book. It was called Eat Less and Move More and it became my first of fifteen best-selling books. I had two other books that I wrote over the next several months. The second book I published was *Motivation 101*, and the third book was called Positivity Attracts. The same thing happened as they also became best-selling books. Other opportunities presented themselves because I wrote those books, published them, and they became best-sellers. Essentially what I was able to do was create the genesis of a book publishing and book-launch marketing system.

Other people took notice, and after my third book became a best-seller then people started reaching out and asking me if I could help them with publishing and marketing their books. That was my role for roughly a year and a half as I was helping people at night with their books and teaching my students during the day.

In June of 2017, I left my teaching position to focus on publishing full time. This is the first part of the pivot. I went from wanting to be a motivational speaker to becoming a publishing and marketing coach. I was helping people with their books and teaching them to use their book as a foundation of their business. Then something changed— and the scary part was this actually happened *after* I left teaching.

What I realized is that a lot of people did not want to learn how to publish and market a book. They didn't. The main thing they kept asking me was if I provided a "done for you" publishing and book-launch marketing service. They just didn't have the time to learn this part of the process. It was a little disheartening, because we had this great coaching program. But then I looked at the math and realized that only a small percentage of people who actually were a part of our program ever finished their book in a timely manner.

We pivoted again, and we made this pivot a little later than expected. For about a year, I struggled with this. I needed to figure out exactly how we could serve our clients, while also helping them get the results they wanted. In December of 2018, I made the decision to shut down the coaching program and focus on "done for you" services.

In 2019, we had our first six-figure year by pivoting. That's the main point I want to emphasize: always listen to your audience. Always listen to your potential clients. If they ask for something then figure out how to provide what they need. That's what we did. Don't be afraid to pivot when the opportunity presents itself.

Listen to your audience, and listen to your clients. If they say that they need something then pivot so you can support them. That's what we did with our "done for you" book publishing and book-launch marketing service. We pivoted, and the main thing now that we help them with is sharing their story. Through this service, we can help them go from just an idea to a best-selling book within ninety days, as long as they are willing to put the work in.

One of the most important things to realize is that you must listen to people. When there is a market, you have to take advantage of it. We did, and when we made that change we had our first six-figure year.

We're now in 2020. Our company is on pace to have another great year. We are able to continue to grow, even with these current times with COVID-19 and everything else that is going on right now in the world. The main reason we have been able to continue to grow is that we already had that online model where we can help people from anywhere in the world.

A lot of people connect with us because of the books that we have out. We have them available in Kindle, paperback, and audiobook, and we have had clients come from all three of those areas. Another thing that we've done is build relationships with other authors in the industry. I have a podcast that we started in 2018 called The Get Published Podcast. It has over 600 episodes currently, and we were able to build relationships with the show. That is what I call my "second pillar of authority.

I refer to our model as the three pillars of authority. They include your book, a podcast, and a virtual summit. We published our first book in 2015. In 2018, we started The Get Published Podcast, and in 2020 we launched our two Get Published Virtual Summits. All three pillars have taken our business to the next level.

Pivoting with that first book and then finding out exactly what other people needed was our start. Over time, our audience kept asking if we could help them with publishing and marketing their book. They had a problem that they needed to solve, so we tailored our business to be able to solve their issues. I can't emphasize that enough. You always want to be solving problems.

Now we focus on our book publishing service and our book-launch marketing service. In addition, we pivoted to now offer a "done for you" virtual summit creation service, which I am doing in a strategic partnership with Ray Brehm.

Ray and I have partnered up to help other people create their own virtual summits—because, again, you want three pillars of authority. You have your book, you have your podcast, and then you have your virtual summit. This doesn't happen overnight. It takes time.

That's the other lesson that I wanted to teach in this chapter: this doesn't happen overnight. You're not going to make a fortune overnight with "get rich quick" schemes. They don't work.

What works is embracing the grind, working hard, and not being afraid to pivot when the opportunity presents itself. I hope this advice helps, because that's exactly what we've done, and it has completely changed our business model for the better.

If you would like some more information about our business, I welcome you to go to www.GetPublishedSystem.com and grab a free copy of my *Get Published* book.

Also on our website, check out The Get Published Podcast. There's also an option on the website to set up a complementary strategy session. I hope I have made it crystal clear that our company has a holistic approach with our strategy sessions. We just want to know how we can help. If we can help you, then we can discuss options. If we can't, we're going to send you some great resources to help you in your journey.

I wish you all the best in your author journey ahead.

You can reach Paul at www.GetPublishedSystem.com.

16

INTUITIVE DECISION MAKING

ERIC TODD JOHNSON, J.D., M.B.A.

Solid decision making, more than any other quality, produces success. Upgrades in decisions always produce improvements. There is a factor in decision making that is available to everyone and that upgrades results.

Intuition can be the first and the last aspect of quality decisions. It is the first when a prompting nudges us to investigate something that otherwise would likely have been left unexplored. It is the last when, after we have considered all other factors and found a decision hanging in the balance, intuition casts a light on our thoughts, illuminating which path to follow.

Intuition, as used here, has little or nothing to do with fancifulness, whimsy, or a roll-of-the-dice. Instead, it is focused on a foundation for solid, pragmatic decisions that regularly produce desired results.

Intuition is not a snap judgment in the absence of facts. Instead, intuition usually grows out of, or is expanded by, gathering and reviewing all facts. This guides us to the edge of what we learn directly from the facts. Having learned all that we can from the facts, we are then in a position to receive and understand the guidance of intuition. Until we comprehend all that the known facts reveal, we are unprepared to understand anything further. It isn't that intuition can never sneak into the equation earlier, but generally such insights remain dormant until after we have explored all that is available to us on a factual basis. It is doubtful that we will be prompted to turn left at an intersection, rather than right, before we arrive at the intersection.

Intuition has long been a sound basis for decisions. Arthur Wellesley is better known as the First Duke of Wellington. He is known for careful military strategies in more than sixty battles, often winning with lesser forces than the enemy. His most notable accomplishment was defeating Napoleon Bonaparte at the battle of Waterloo. Later, he served as prime minister of the British Empire. With life and death literally hanging in the balance, he did nothing rashly, nor whimsically. Yet, the Duke of Wellington acknowledged the impact of intuition in his decisions, as follows:

"There is a curious thing that one feels sometimes; when you are considering a subject, suddenly a whole train of reasoning comes before like a flash of light; you see it all (moving his hand as if something appeared before him, his eye with the brightest expression), yet it takes you perhaps two years to put on paper all that has occurred to your mind in an instant. Every part of the subject, the bearing of all the parts upon each other, and all the consequences are there before you."

— (ELIZABETH LONGFORD, *WELLINGTON, PILLAR OF STATE*, P. 506).

This description by the Duke of Wellington is ripe with insights and rife with meaning. A person can hardly expect such a "flash of light" unless and until they have traveled to the edge of what is already known. A key to that element of judgment born of intuition is to have mastered the known field and then to contemplate what may lie beyond.

The Duke of Wellington captures another key to increasing inspiration. It is important that we pay attention to and apply such insights. He mentions putting on paper all that occurred to his mind. Writing down and retaining these important moments enables us to more fully follow and apply our insights accurately. The simple act of writing our thoughts demonstrates our willingness to comply. Also, because memories fade all too quickly, a written record helps us continue to comply over time.

A written record can have another important impact, especially where the insight may be less concrete than that described by the Duke of Wellington. Not all impressions are received with equal force. When we record a less dramatic impression, we can later consult it. To our happy surprise, we may discover that what seemed at the time to be but a reasonable possibility, a hope, has actually matured into a series of direct events in our lives. Reviewing our written impressions can help us identify the feeling associated with those impressions, which in turn can help us better grasp or recognize future impressions and gain greater benefit from them.

The Duke of Wellington describes a whole train of reasoning that occurred to his mind. This is a wonderful description. At times, we may receive an entire train of insight.

On other occasions, the insight may dawn upon our minds one train car at a time. This presents another good reason to transcribe our impressions. When we only glimpse a single train car of insight, recording such thoughts and pondering what else may apply is an excellent way to invite additional train cars of insight. As we sense and respond to each train car of insight, more and more train cars are brought to our attention, until over time the entire train of insight is finally brought before our view.

When inspiration arrives one train car at a time, it can be tempting to question whether the thought or idea is worth pursuing. Here is an exercise to help sort out when we should persist with a train of thought, or turn to something else.

If we sense a spark, the first thing to do is to act on that spark. We should do what we can to implement it and follow through. Because we have only received a single train car of inspiration—only a nudge, so to speak—it is doubtful that the full impact in our lives will be felt immediately. Instead, we may sense a buoyant feeling that seems to enlarge our thoughts and feelings related to the spark. We may feel that our understanding is enlightened. We may gain a sense of satisfaction, almost as if something tasted delicious to us. Following such thoughts leads to additional insights.

There are many other strong reasons to write our impressions, keeping them in a secure place away from intrusion. One of these is to help us retain our humility. Without question, the insights mentioned by the Duke of Wellington are akin to our own thoughts. They are of the same nature and substance. Accordingly, it is exceedingly easy for us to mistake such intuitions for our own thoughts. When we make this mistake, ugly pride enters. Writing our impressions can help us recognize another source: their true source.

Intuition comes to those who give their all. Slackers and curiosity seekers need not apply. As a general rule, intuition and inspiration are the privilege of the fully committed. The partially committed, those who only seem to want guidance when they are in a pickle, may find that their access to insight is clouded by anxiousness.

Perhaps sharing a personal example of intuition will help shed light on this subject. I am a lawyer. As a law student, I vaulted from dead last in my class to first in my class. Intuition played a key role.

In preparing for exams for my first semester of law school, one professor told the class that he would draw a question from prior exams, and that he kept copies of the prior exams on file in the library. My study group copied all of his prior exams and reviewed them. Our last night studying before the test, we reviewed the test questions from the prior exams. We would each take a turn outlining an answer to a test question for the rest of the group, and then the group would give their feedback on the answer. When my turn came to outline an answer, the question dealt with the proper jurisdiction for handling a dispute over child custody between unmarried parents living in different states. I outlined an answer. My friends in the study group added their input and we felt that we had crafted a rather good answer.

The next morning on the exam, halfway through the test, this same question was presented. I smiled to myself and began writing furiously. I already knew exactly how I would answer. As I was completing this answer, however, a thought struck me. It was something the professor had mentioned once in passing. It was a factor that would change my conclusion. As soon as this thought popped into my mind, it was clear that the best analysis needed to include this factor.

Accordingly, I erased portions of my exam answer, inserted an analysis with this new factor, and completed my answer, which now had a different conclusion. At the moment, it struck me as curious that this factor should pop into my mind during the exam, when it hadn't occurred to me or anyone in my study group when we were preparing and had ample time to consider all angles to the question.

Now let me turn to the practical and pragmatic results that intuition can prompt. I received a perfect score on the exam question. Later, I learned that this professor had previously litigated the exact child custody question that he put on the test. And guess what? My professor won his lawsuit based on the additional factor that popped into my mind as I was completing my answer. This professor was a nationally renowned expert in family law. Contrary to the answer that I had prepared before the test, the answer that ended up on my exam mirrored the exact argument he presented in court and on which he won his case.

My highest grade in law school was in this class. Despite the fact that I began law school dead last in my class, to my great surprise, I literally rose from worst to first. At the end of the first semester of law school, I was told that I was number one in my class.

I could easily say that it was my own thought during the exam that carried the day. But I know in my heart-of-hearts that I had no intention of discussing that additional factor. I was wrapping up my answer, exactly the way I had prepared it earlier with my study group. I even had a small bubble of pride about my pre-prepared answer. I wasn't pausing to contemplate whether I should add anything or say something different. The additional factor crowded into my mind. Intuition made all the difference.

Inspiration, intuition, insight—call it what you will—is a legitimate element of sound judgment. Our judgment is enhanced when we notice such "stray" thoughts and implement them in our lives.

I should note that this helpful thought only came to me after full preparation. While the thought came to my mind, it wasn't exclusively my thought. If it had been, it would have occurred to me when I answered the question the night before the exam with my study group.

Sound judgment is the distinguishing quality for lawyers. Sound judgment is also the distinguishing quality for every successful person in every field. Everyone can build better judgment and everyone will prosper by doing so. Effective preparation and sound experience in the matter at hand are hallmarks of sound judgment. Taking time to understand the various factors that impact a decision is important. While we may feel pressure to arrive at an answer promptly, if additional information is needed for a fully informed decision, then we are wise to wait. Finally, our best judgment takes into account not just intellectual information, but our feelings and additional intuition as well. The practical advantages of doing so cannot be overlooked.

17

NICELY SUCCESSFUL

LISA MCNAIR PALMER, ESQ.

I grew up with four sisters and our mother was always, always, always telling us to "be nice." I got so sick of hearing her say that. It was her answer for everything. If someone was rude to you on the school bus, you were supposed to be nice. If someone said they did not like your shirt, you were supposed to be nice. We were supposed to go through life being kind to everyone. This lesson has seemed somewhat controversial and quaint at some points in my life.

My mother is, and always has been, one of the nicest people you will ever meet. She is a role model for many and an all-around great lady. She came from a very large family and has suffered her share of hard times. She had to overcome many challenges, but remained nice through every one of them.

She and my dad ran a small farm and they worked so hard as I was growing up. We lived in "Tornado Alley," and sometimes the storms would tear up our trees and our garden after we had put in tons of effort to grow fruits and vegetables so our family would have food all year. She canned vegetables and helped my dad vaccinate cattle and deliver calves. She helped build fences and form strong bonds with neighbors. Through it all, she was (and still is) a nice person. "You girls be nice," was a mantra in our house.

I followed my mom's advice growing up, and my childhood was great. Being nice (at least most of the time) worked out well for me. Niceness is ingrained in me, because that sort of programming sticks with you. I felt a bit of resentment at the fact that I sometimes held my tongue when I could have retorted and had the last word. I could have embarrassed a classmate whose skirt had ridden up, but instead I quietly pointed it out to her before anyone else noticed. I could have refused to help my cousin with homework, but he asked nicely so I assisted him. I remained quiet when I could have assessed blame for a mistake by someone else. I learned to listen a lot when someone needed to be heard.

When I went off to college and began to seek success away from home, I struggled with the idea that in order to get ahead, I just could *not* be nice all the time. This was unsettling, because being nice was my default setting. When I decided my junior year at university that I wanted to become a lawyer, I just knew my mom's advice to "be nice" was never going to work if I wanted to be a success.

Cognitive dissonance raised its ugly head. How could my beliefs and attitude about always being kind play out in the "real" world of a successful legal career? I planned to become a litigator—a trial lawyer. How could I follow the "Golden Rule" and still become a silver-tongued attorney? Hard-hitting cross examination and persuading juries did not leave much room for niceness. Or so I thought.

My first job out of law school was with a big, respected law firm in Austin, Texas. I became part of the "litigation section." I carefully watched the top lawyers in the firm strut their stuff in the courtroom, and I observed the tactics of opposing counsel as well. These lawyers worked for big, rich companies and important, influential people. I was a small cog in a big wheel, but I paid attention.

The top litigator in our firm was an important figure in the state's bar association and was regularly named one of the top one hundred lawyers in the United States. He was brilliant, tall, and distinguished. He could charm birds out of trees and CEOs out of huge sums of money. Juries loved him, other lawyers tried their best to outwit him, and I was privileged to learn from him. He did not flaunt his intelligence, never talked down to anyone, and was fun and friendly. And, most surprisingly, he was *nice*. He seemed to actually prioritize being nice to everyone, no matter their status or what they could do for him. Unbelievable.

I kept watching for shades of evil, for the diabolical side to this man, my boss and mentor. I never saw anything like that from him, even under extreme pressure. During sensitive negotiations, I saw him offer to go get coffee for his opposition. When he was frivolously sued for malpractice, he did not lash out at people he could have blamed; he searched for solutions and worked at building up the confidence of the people around him. Had my mom been talking to him? This guy's niceness was not an impediment to his success; it was a huge, key asset. Mind blown. Repeatedly.

After five years of law practice with this firm and mentor, I moved into successful solo law practice. By that time, it had finally settled into my bones, my brain, and my heart that my natural inclination to be nice was an incredible asset. My mother's constant reminders provided success on a farm, at school, in personal relationships, with colleagues, and in a courtroom. Being nice wins. Everywhere.

Being nice really is crucial to a successful life. We each define what success means to us. To me, success has to do with peace of mind, love, respect, contentment, and a sufficient amount of money to do and be and have what I need and want. I have had a wonderful life with very few regrets, and I attribute much of this to my mother's admonition to always be nice.

I have a fantastic family, I love my work, I make plenty of money, I'm a published author of many works, I indulge my love of travel, I have ride-or-die friends, and I sleep well at night. I am happy and content. This is success. Success does not cause happiness—it is the other way around. Happiness, contentment, and knowing you treat people well causes success. Being nice leads to authentic connections with people who want to spend time with you, support you, have fun with you, and do business with you. You are more likely to achieve your goals by being nice; in other words (and this is something else my mom says), "you catch more flies with honey than with vinegar."

Kindness breeds confidence and comfort in your own skin. Despite what you may have heard, nice guys finish *first*. Nice people win, and they make winners of the people around them. How many times have you heard, "You have to give to get?" or, "What goes around comes around?" Being nice and giving the best of yourself means that others want to help you. And they want what you have. There is a certain charisma that comes with the inner knowledge that you have treated others in the right way.

Someone I know will read this and think "Well, she wasn't very nice to me on January 27, 2015!" Of course, it is impossible to be nice one hundred percent of the time. And sometimes you are not perceived as nice when you draw necessary boundaries for your own good or the good of someone else. Being nice does not equal being a doormat. It does not mean losing. It does not mean a lack of boundaries. It involves showing the same attitude toward yourself that you show to other people.

Sometimes, being kind to yourself is the path to sanity in an insane world. Your kindness to yourself will spill over to the people around you. Being nice to yourself means that *you* get to choose how you spend your time, with whom you spend it, and how you treat the people in your life. At the end of your days, would you rather have been an example of a nice person or a crotchety old person?

A cranky colleague said to me once, years ago, "How do you do it? It's like you have this light shining out all around you and you just go through life being so nice, and everything works out for you." Let the light of your own particular brand of niceness shine. Others will notice.

Sometimes being nice means giving my time, talents, and money without expecting anything in return. It means showing respect and listening to others' points of view. It involves treating others the way I want to be treated. As a disability lawyer, I have learned over the years that my clients are usually in pain, be it physical or mental, and they can be aggressive and downright mean at times. Though it may not be easy, I meet their harsh attitude with kindness. I remind my staff that, while we never put up with verbal abuse, we give our clients an extra measure of tolerance. If anyone needs us to be nice, it is a client who can no longer work and may be losing their home and their family because life has not gone as planned. It is important to strive to be nice to everyone, and to keep in mind that some people need an extra dose of kindness.

Meeting anger with kindness can put an instant damper on a bad temper. Children react better when you decline to escalate, as do lawyers, judges, and hostile witnesses. Niceness contributes to a desired lack of drama and can prevent pot-stirring by those who love trouble. Starting with niceness can work wonders with bosses and coworkers, friends and strangers. The more you practice kindness, the easier it becomes to stay "nicely successful."

How would your life be different if you treated everyone with kindness? In writing this chapter, I looked for quotes from successful lawyers, writers, business leaders, and entrepreneurs having to do with success and being nice. In my brief online research, I did not find any such quotes—maybe because being nice is a quiet skill that brings results in an almost sneaky way. I found no quotes, but I have lost track of the number of times I have heard successful people say that they got to where they are by helping others. Good things started happening when they started giving. That is really just a way of saying they were nice to others, which helped them, in turn, become successful.

It took a while, but I have discovered that my mother, who has never given a motivational speech, led a large organization, closed a multimillion-dollar deal, or convinced a jury she was right, gave me the best advice I've ever received for how to survive and thrive in every situation. Yes—work hard, be hungry, educate yourself, and hit it hard to achieve your dreams. I have done all that, and continue to do it—but the key is that I have always remembered to "be nice," just like my mama told me.

18

RUN YOUR OWN RACE

LESLIE OLMO

I am really excited to offer a fundamental piece of advice that will contribute to your success.

As communicators, we often begin by sharing our own stories so our audience can be confident we will be worth their time. I love to share funny stories about my experiences, but I want this chapter to be about you. If I start telling you all about myself, it may help you relate to me, but you will start comparing what I have done—good or bad—with who you are and what you have done. We can hardly keep ourselves from considering someone's advice without comparing ourselves to them. I want to make sure that while you are reading, you are thinking about yourself. I believe I am offering you valuable advice, so I hope you will keep reading!

We begin to reach for "success" from a very early age. This is a natural consequence of our learning processes from infancy through adulthood. We learn new tasks, improve our skills, and receive feedback in abundance! This creates an ongoing feedback loop. Each success is represented by an acquired skill or an increase in knowledge. Basically, a lesson is learned. I believe the original connotation of success was related to the simple achievement of a desired outcome. I do not believe the original meaning of success included the level of personal emotional attachment that the word seems to convey today.

At some point, our abundant feedback loop gets out of whack. We begin to experience anxiety about the feedback that will come next. For no apparent reason, we start to doubt that we will be able to handle our next lesson. We start to look around ourselves to see if other people are successfully handling the challenges we are expecting. When we see others completing these lessons, we determine that we need to be like them to be successful. This literally changes the definition of success! Success starts to become a human characteristic instead of simply indicating that a particular objective has been achieved at a point in time.

Based on what others are accomplishing, we begin to assign time frames, deadlines, and variations in the quality and quantity of output to the lessons we hope to complete. We assign so many parameters that we can only "hope" to complete the next lesson. The lesson is no longer one lesson; it is many lessons combined into one. This decreases the chance of completing the lesson at all. No completion means no success, which means failure. And the doubt just continues to grow.

We have turned the feedback loop into a negative loop. We begin to reevaluate ourselves and our success through the eyes of other people and in relation to other people. Notice I did not say "evaluate;" I said "reevaluate." We decide that our evaluation of ourselves is most likely flawed, and we, too, are therefore flawed.

New ideas creep in. Success is no longer the simple completion of a desired task or outcome. To be successful, you must complete the task and complete it quickly. You must go above and beyond what was expected so everyone notices. This will get you a better job than the next guy, and in the end you will get the promotion and the raise. I realize this example is a little over-simplified, but there it is. Everything about success just became about money!

Now, before anyone gets upset, I have no problem with money. I like money just like everyone else, but it is not the measure of my success. Money is the outcome of applying the lessons we learn, but it does not determine if we have been successful. Otherwise, there would be no unhappy rich people. If you take a look at the internet and social media, you will find a *lot* of unhappy rich people.

Honestly, you need to understand that you are already and always have been successful. You may not feel that way, but imagine the millions of lessons you have learned in your lifetime. Each of those is a success. Life is not easy. You are successful. Learning to use a spoon is a success—imagine if you had skipped this step!

So, how would you describe the success that you are hoping to achieve by learning some of the lessons in this book? Let's start with some basic ideas about success. There are two primary ideas: the materialistic and the idealistic. Most definitions go something like this, whether we want to admit it or not.

- Materialistic Success: The attainment of money, job titles, material items, and fame will lead to a life of love, peace, and happiness.
- Idealistic Success: Living a life of love, peace, and happiness will lead you to attain money, job titles, material items, and fame.

You can see that these definitions include the same elements. If asked, we would most likely offer a variation of the second definition —just so we would not appear to be shallow!

The truth is that all of those benefits are perfectly legitimate motivators. Other people might be looking for healthy relationships, fulfilled dreams, or the ability to check items off a bucket list. The issue is not which motivators are acceptable. The issue is whether you think a certain level of attainment is essential to your success.

Most of us have a general idea of what we would like to accomplish before we feel able to determine that we are officially successful. This list of accomplishments is made up of many smaller accomplishments along the way. So, how will you know when you have accomplished your ultimate success?

Simply checking tasks and achievements off a list will not satisfy today's definition of success. The concept of success implies that success will be satisfying, but often, that is not the case. There is a disconnect between the elements of success. Why is this? Today's version of success is really an intangible concept, yet we try to tie it to tangible results. This leads us to a more materialistic definition of success. But if the concept of success is truly intangible, each of us is required to define it for ourselves. Because of the intangible nature of success, we do not believe we have achieved success until we *feel* successful. I believe you can only *feel* successful when you achieve a certain *satisfaction* in the desired outcome.

So, how do you achieve this satisfactory success? You must *"Run Your Own Race!"* No matter what. This is easier said than done. The concept is simple enough, but it will require a lot of your time, energy, and honesty.

I want to start by considering what keeps us from running our own race. Remember that whole, out-of-whack feedback loop? To run your own race, you need to understand one thing: *Comparison is The Root of All Evil.* I love to say that because it sounds dramatic, and it's easy to remember!

Comparison. We do this in every circumstance, every job, every relationship, and everything else! Not all comparison is bad, but all of our negative evaluations begin with an inaccurate comparison of some kind. Stop and think about this. How many times have you been disappointed in your results when you decided you wanted to do something or be something based on observing someone else— someone you thought was "successful?"

That is exhausting and discouraging. While comparison itself is not evil, all evil seems to begin with comparison. Literally, all the way back to the beginning of mankind! This isn't a discussion about faith, but it is interesting that in this old literary work called "the Bible," this theme of comparison as evil permeates the stories and messages. Remember the snake? He impacted Eve's actions by suggesting that she compare herself to God.

Bad move, but that's for another story! The point is that the earliest stories in various histories and cultures document the heartbreak and sorrow for those who live by this type of comparison. This theme remains prevalent in many of today's books and movies. And yet, we still do it.

There are great reasons to periodically evaluate ourselves and our circumstances, but too often, the results of this type of exercise are overwhelmingly negative. Our primary motivation for change occurs when we perceive that someone else appears to meet our misguided definition of success. We initiate changes based solely on these observations and do not consider other essential factors. When we fall into this trap, our inability to achieve someone else's idea of success causes great emotional harm and distress. This type of comparison does not lead to more success. If you aren't sure about this, take another look at the internet and social media.

You must run your own race.

I like to define "Run Your Own Race" this way:

Run: Run implies moving in a forward direction, making forward progress. It implies movement, but not at a certain speed. The destination is not indicated. So, while running is essential, running alone will not bring you satisfactory success.

Your: It's *your* race, so it should be inspired by yourself. There are too many kinds of races. I cannot imagine you would want to participate in all of them, unless of course, you are an Ironman. Plus it's "run your own *race*," not "run your own *races*!" You must choose.

Own: Yep, you are going to have to own it! You need to choose something sustainable for which you can remain accountable.

Race: A race indicates some kind of journey from point A to point B. While running does not dictate speed, the word race implies you are aware of the need to keep a decent pace. A race has a defined finish line. Without a predetermined finish line, you will never complete your race.

There you have it: *Run Your Own Race!*

The difficulty comes in evaluating all those pieces of the puzzle. (I know; it's a race and not a puzzle!) We need to proactively utilize the tools available to us to discern the race we would like to run. If you believe you have done this and are still experiencing extreme disappointment or distress, this indicates that something in your decision chain is not working for you. You just need to back up—you ran too fast! If you invest the time and continue to evaluate and make necessary adjustments, I guarantee you will have a certain satisfaction in the outcome.

There you have it: *Satisfying Success!*

Here is the good news: you *can* be anything. There is a training program, an education program, or an online course for everything under the sun. If you can follow a road map, you can do it. The key is to choose wisely.

You will need to gather the necessary tools to help you draft your vision for success. Learning to use comparison positively will help you clarify your desires and create a set of defined values. You will begin to build a framework through which you will validate your choices. A proactive approach to surrounding yourself with mentors and those you can trust will help you refine your plans. Investing in industry-specific training and education will ensure you are confident and prepared.

Continuing to develop character traits and skills furthers the ability to achieve your vision. Prioritize your efforts based on your own strengths and weaknesses. Read more books like this one! Watch videos and take advantage of other online resources to increase your competence. Choose from topics like motivation, mindset, organizational skills, SMART goals, communication, self-esteem, relationships, and how to determine your "why." Pay attention to your physical and mental health needs. The list of resources is endless. Just don't forget to pace yourself—it's a race, but not a sprint!

I am working to complete my book on this topic, and the title will be, of course, *Run Your Own Race*. I am developing worksheets and resources by chapter that will walk readers through the entire evaluation process. I would love to gather your input and feedback as the project evolves. If you have an interest in receiving advance chapters and worksheets in exchange for input and feedback, I invite you to join my Race Team online at www.leslieolmo.com.

My chapter is coming to a close, and I was able to refrain from telling a bunch of goofy stories about myself. However, it is time for me to share something about myself that really sums up my message to you.

I am so successful that I can wear my shorts, t-shirts, and flip flops everywhere I go!

I have decided that I have the freedom to do that. Is it great for every situation—like landing a corporate job? No. But, I don't really want a corporate job anymore. They say you should dress for the job you want. Luckily, I just want to be myself. I honestly love to wear shorts, t-shirts, and flip flops. That's it. The inner me shows through. Wearing happy clothes makes me happy, which helps me make better decisions on my way to achieving satisfying success.

This is the key phrase: I have decided that I have the freedom to do that!

That makes me feel successful.

This is my sincere hope for you: *I hope that you can decide that you have that same kind of freedom!* No, you do not have to dress like me to do it.

Here's to your satisfying success!

Leslie can be found online at www.leslieolmo.com.

19

STRENGTH-BASED SUCCESS

DR. KANNA KRISHNAN LLB HONS(UK) MBA HRM (AUS) DBA(SWIT)

Over the past twenty years, I have climbed to the top-notch position as both generalist Human Resource personnel and specialized regional training and development position in two national and seven multinational companies. I thought I had become a very successful professional, but I lost everything one day and I had to search for success all over again.

Let me start by giving you my credentials and my fall. Upon the completion of my degree in law and after attending thirty-eight job interviews, I ended up getting a position in a Cineplex as a cinema attendant. I graduated just in time for the rescission to set in. It kicked my dreams of becoming a lawyer to the curb. I needed to start making money to sustain myself; I was twenty-five and still living with my parents.

Adamantly, I started working hard, and on my initiative I was training newcomers to the job. My superior recognised my initiative and appointed me to be the company's first Training Executive. That was my first breakthrough to the corporate ladder. I trained the Cineplex managers and front line employees, who were placed all over the country. Having reached the highest position in the company and winning the best customer service award for training program implementation, I took the next step and became a Training Manager at Equatorial Hotel in the highlands.

From the hospitality industry, I moved to another conglomerate and worked in Friesland Cobercco, Pfizer, UPM Raflatac, Kimberly Clarke, and later AM Metlife. Nothing stopped my climb. At the end of my climb, I was in one of the top ten Biopharma companies in the world as their Senior Human Resource Director. This is considered to be one of the most senior positions in the entire human resource field.

I was at the peak, but suddenly I started to lose everything. The pressure of being in the top position, the tiredness of climbing the corporate ladder, and the emptiness inside of me began to take a toll. It affected my personal life and my family life. Whatever I acquired progressively started to disintegrate away, right before my eyes. Every relationship got lesser day by day.

I often started to cry in solitude and started to believe that perhaps I was not mentally well—as my loved ones often mentioned before leaving. Believing those words, I went to the psychiatrist for a diagnosis. While the results showed that I was undergoing a traumatic period, I was deemed fine and not mentally insane, as assumed by others around me. Hence started the most difficult phase of my life which was learning to know and healing myself.

The simplest thing I could do at that time was drawing, so I started the positive art therapy course that I purchased for a loved one. Surprisingly, it helped me to develop my vision board for the future, my new future. My love for positive psychology was planted that day and from that moment onward, I applied the scientific, research-based methodologies of a self-growth mindset, corporate development, and spiritual wellbeing. It was the birth of the new ME.

With this understanding on how to find and use my character strength for success, I completed a Positive Psychology Coach Certificate and, later, a Positive Workplace Change Agent certification from the Netherlands, as well as completing my doctorate. By utilizing positive psychology at the workplace, I built my human resources team from five to fifteen employees whilst garnering a Best Workplace Award and an Innovation in Recruitment Award in the biopharma industry.

This made me decide to embark on my consultancy practice, Positive Corporate Consulting. Then, I decided to coach others on the secret of success, utilizing positive psychology by incorporating Positive Success Coaching. That success helped me win the IEBA Entrepreneur Award for my business endeavour.

Today, I am optimizing my exposure both globally and locally in building thriving, positive people and flourishing corporations. I am continuing to do scholarly research to expand my knowledge in corporate management development, toward developing positive personalities, leaderships, and flourishing positive institutions. My success was only due to identifying and utilizing my character strengths based on positive psychology. I realized that, even if you are able to achieve all your personal and professional goals, if they are not congruent with or not utilizing your endowed character strengths, you will not feel successful. It will therefore be difficult to flourish in your wellbeing (my new indicator for success).

I started to focus on how to use my strengths instead of trying to improve my weaknesses. To my surprise, I realized my breakdown was due to over-using my signature strengths. Based on a VIA scientific assessment I undertook (which you will also be able to do, as I have shown the method below), my first character strength was identified as "Love Of Learning," referring to the desire for learning for learning's sake. Once I understood this, I started to learn about positive psychology to help me out of my depressive state. I learned everything from the experts and started to use these lessons in my daily life.

Today, I am using the same science to learn how to help others by coaching them on positive psychology interventions. Positive psychology taught me to identify my character's blind spots, which were my tendency to overwhelm others with information overload and getting frustrated when they do not understand me. Thus, I have since learned to give pause and obtain constructive feedback from others. I have also mastered the arts of active listening and listening unconditionally.

Success became more frequent when I transferred my tasks into meaningful goals and found how to be in flow while putting in effort. Once I learned how to spot strengths in others, I started to coach others to identify their strengths and utilize them to achieve their successes as well. Strength spotting is a positive psychology character strength identification based on the words, behaviours, and communications of others. This will help us influence and communicate with others, as we can be aligned and synergize to their character strengths for task completion. Consequently, I took the opportunity to coach them on resilience (ability to cope with what life throws at you), developing grit (powerful motivation to fulfil one's desires), and perseverance (finish what you start) until they achieved success in their vocation.

Once this was successful, I tried applying this philosophy to business organizations by introducing strength-based strategy planning and developing positive managers and positive leadership, as well as creating a positive workplace. This worked remarkably well. Strength-based strategy planning, unlike the traditional SWOT analysis, does not focus on weakness and threat. The Positive Manager program focuses on strength-based competency that is needed for the manager to lead in all types of management models. Positive Leadership focuses on how the leaders of a business can proactively utilise strengths towards developing a company that thrives positively. I started to realize that organizations prefer to engage employees who are utilizing a strength-based model rather than weakness-based, performance-improvement model.

This is when I decided to dedicate myself to the development of the positive institution in the corporate world. It is my calling and profession in life. If you would like to achieve success in whatever endeavour or undertaking you wish, the following steps will be helpful based on positive psychology approach:

1. List domains of life or areas of business that you would like to be successful in by utilizing The Wheel of Life (you could Google this term if it is unfamiliar to you).
2. Prioritize it on a scale of one to ten. How meaningful do you find these areas in your life? Focus on those with a higher score.
3. Identify your signature strength for FREE at https://www.viacharacter.org/survey/account/register via Value in Action Strength Survey.
4. Realize the top three are your signature strengths. Do not focus on the last five in the report that you will receive after your assessment is completed.
5. Now, look at your signature character strength in the assessment and consider how you can utilize it in the area you identified as your topmost priority.
6. Identify whether you are overusing, not using, OR created a blind spot while using this strength in this area.
7. Next, identify how you could develop perseverance and be in flow while focusing on the task you would like to be successful in doing.
8. Create a vision board of the result (preferable have ONE graphic representation) of the goals in mind that you identified. The more appealing it is, the better impact it will have on you subconsciously.
9. Next, create a SMART goal on how to use your signature strength to achieve your goals and review them periodically (daily, weekly, monthly, or quarterly).
10. Finally, on a daily basis, record in your gratitude journal the small successes achieved for that day. It might be hard in the beginning, but do not end the day without accepting small successes and being thankful about it!

Be positive! Success will be yours.

You can connect with Dr. Kanna at: positivesuccesscoach.com

20

HABITUAL IMPLEMENTATION

BRAD JOHNSON

I didn't always know I wanted to be a writer.

In fact, if you had asked me what my goals were as a teenager, I would have probably only replied, "be in a touring band full-time." That vision was valuable to me, but not nearly as valuable as what I'd learn through countless instances of trial and error.

Little did I know that over the next few years, the entire way I viewed making a living, and the attitudes necessary for it, would be flipped 180 degrees.

I remember a time when I thought writing was cool for those who liked it, but I didn't find personal joy in it, and certainly didn't think of it as a career—much less a career where I could call my own shots.

Close to a decade ago, in looking for ways to financially supplement my personal music dreams, I realized writing is an incredible way to share your thoughts with others, help them succeed, and also make money.

I also quickly realized that writing is not for the unmotivated, uninitiated, or unprepared. The articles, blogs, and videos I began poring over painted a clear picture of the fruits of a writing career, but not always the strategies necessary to get there. Silly me figured if

I simply started pounding out words on a keyboard, eventually I'd get where I wanted to be...wherever *that* was.

That mindset turned out to be partly true, and partly false.

Forging ahead with determination and little else, I launched my blog during the summer of 2013. Much to my joy, a few hundred friends and contacts checked it out during launch week, which kept me motivated. I quickly fell in love with the content creation process and knew that if I wanted to see results, I simply had to be persistent. I continued to churn out blog posts and put fingers to keys on my keyboard and thought I was getting somewhere.

As I delved into the worlds of Amazon, email marketing, SEO, and more, I faced what every honest writer will admit they've asked themselves at one point: "Am I a good enough writer? Was I meant for this?"

Seeing author after author release their books on Amazon or launch their own products had me second-guessing my own drive. Throwing in the towel somehow became appealing.

Facing up against the sheer volume of content available today was a factor that nearly knocked me out, too. I remember thinking about the incredible books I had already read, my growing to-read list. With so many insightful writers already out there, I couldn't grasp how I could have anything useful to offer that hadn't already been said.

Even on great days when ideas seemed to flow effortlessly, it felt like the world's eyes were always bearing down on me, criticizing every action I thought was worthwhile. I still remember oscillating between whether or not I should publish my first book, and what people would think of me and my writing. If you've wanted to write or are on the journey of writing, too, you may be nodding your head as you think about your own obstacles.

I discovered I had to silence my inner critic and felt all the better for it. With criticism gone and new days ahead, I kept plugging away. As various people in my life asked what I was up to, I let them know that I was working on more books on my journey to becoming a full-time writer. The mixed responses I received produced a mental cloud of confusion and disorientation that knocked me off track.

I had quit my previous job to focus on writing full-time around the time I had launched my blog, in the summer of 2013. The months that ensued had their rewards, but they had many trials and failures as well.

The better part of a year later, I was on the verge of tears. My freelance writing client pool had dried up, my existing work wasn't paying well, and I was forced to pick up a retail job to keep afloat. I came face to face with painful, yet essential lessons that I carry with me to this day in my writing career.

It wasn't until I sat down—months after this hiccup—and decided exactly what I wanted to do that I realized I needed clarity and real help. My voyage into uncharted waters of personal passion taught me that blind ambition alone does not yield the characteristics or behaviors necessary for success.

I learned that success is not just about one action or "hack." Rather, success is **about proper, habitual implementation of the** *correct* **actions.**

It's not about haphazardly putting together a strategy and hoping it works. It's about examining what works for others and replicating those same processes for your own audience and work.

I used the strategies and mindsets I'm about to share with you to launch chart-topping Amazon Kindle books, write popular posts for established self-development sites, amass over 860,000 views for my Quora content, and more.

1. Establish a clear strategy.

As tempting as it is to believe you can start at square one and figure everything out on your own as you go, the use of a thought-out strategy will get you the results you want much more easily. And I don't mean you should be dreaming up a strategy on your own, either. Here's a secret: **if someone is successful with anything, it means they've mastered a replicable process that achieves their desired outcome.** The well-established 80/20 rule teaches us that only twenty percent of your efforts yield eighty percent of your results, and anyone with a worthwhile strategy has identified that twenty percent of their actions which are "high impact" efforts. Every role model you have for your own goals has separated high-impact activities from low-impact ones. It's essential to mirror this type of action for your own results.

In the same way that you can't rely on reaching a travel destination without some kind of map, you aren't going to be where you want to be in business without completing actions that manifest growth-oriented cycles. For example, if you want to be selling more copies of your book on Amazon, building an email list of readers is a better plan than simply putting your book up for sale and hoping readers buy it, also called "hope marketing." This is something I learned the hard way, but ever since I've changed my strategy, I've seen improved results.

The exact strategy you employ depends on your goal, business model, consumer desires, and needs in your market. A great way to build a legitimate strategy from scratch is to reverse engineer the methodologies of leaders in your niche. Open up your favorite spreadsheet software and use the following approach:

A) In the top row, list the top three or four people who are absolutely crushing it in your market. With each in a separate column, break down the following:

1. What marketing strategies do they talk about frequently? Are there methods that work well for them? (Label this: Top Marketing Strategies)
2. What types of content are they producing? Which pieces of their content get the highest engagement levels (likes, shares, comments, related articles)? (Label this: Best-Performing Content)
3. How can you produce similar content for **your** audience? (Label this: Similar Content for My Audience)
4. What strategies are they using to grow their email list?

How can you employ this (or a low-budget version, if funds are limited)? (Label this: List Building Strategies)

5. As you add information to the sheet, you can color code similar cells for easier visual digestion of what you've added. To learn how to use conditional formatting, go here: https://bit.ly/conditionalFormatting

6. If need be, simply insert rows between people when you add new entries.

7. **Use these discoveries to initiate your core growth cycle in your business.**

B) Make five new columns in your spreadsheet, and label them the following:

1. Frequency to Implement (Weekly, bi-weekly, daily, etc.)
2. Time Required
3. Tech Tools Required
4. Research Required
5. Funds Required
6. Under each column, review the cell entries from columns in section A, and identify what the appropriate entry is per need.
7. **Use your entries to solidify your plan, remain focused, prevent getting overwhelmed, and allocate resources efficiently.** Your time, energy, and money are all valuable —you should treat them as such!

C) Make five new columns in your spreadsheet, and label them the following:

1. Traffic
2. Audience and Relationship Building
3. Product or Service Creation

4. Content Creation
5. Vanity Metrics (optional). This is for anything like social media likes, podcast downloads, article shares, etc.
6. When the columns are made, use data validation to turn the cells into checkboxes. To learn how to use data validation, go here: https://bit.ly/dataValidation
7. Simply check the according box if an action pertains to it, e.g. a Facebook ad is Traffic; a social media post is Content Creation.

After your spreadsheet work is done, it's important to evaluate it against the backdrop of your real business. In other words, what worked at a larger scale for someone else may need to be adjusted for your current place in business. A thousand-dollar course another pro sold to their audience of 45,000 may or may not be what your audience needs right now, but that doesn't mean you can't glean a habit from it. Take the information you've discovered and adapt it to what your business and audience need.

To know if your new strategy is relevant to your business, these are some questions to ask yourself:

- Is X action addressing my audience's pain points or making a solution for them?
- Am I able to grow a stronger, more engaged audience because of X?
- Is X contributing to a sales offer my audience wants or needs?
- Is X making it easier and more inviting for my audience members to engage?
- Is X helping my audience members succeed?

2. Afford dedicated commitment in your calendar for your goals.

It cannot be overstated that personal time commitment is one of, if not *the*, largest factor in success for any venture. If you haven't carved out consistent time in your schedule for your goals and dreams, you owe it to yourself to do so.

The particular day and amount of time you spend is not as important as it being habitual. If Saturday mornings are your preference, then rock it. If Tuesday evenings are better, more power to you. Whether you spend thirty minutes, an hour, or two hours whenever you sit down to work, use a time block that works for you and brings you closer to your goals. But make it consistent.

3. Learn about necessary growth habits from those who have gone before you.

In addition to fully committing to your goals and building your strategy, learning from those who have already become successful in what you want to do is the most reliable fast track to success. Buying courses from people you know, like, and trust is valuable—as long as you implement the course. Joining an email list for a free case study download is useful—as long as you read the case study. You can uncover nearly infinite amounts from those who have already mastered worthwhile habits and actions in your arena, as long as you maintain follow-through after learning. Action is everything.

4. Create foundational wins—quickly.

A writer friend of mine, Aram, introduced me to his concept of "foundational wins" a few years ago. This is closely related to the reality that at some point, you're going to face a career-related obstacle that you feel is insurmountable. Whether it's launching a new product, growing your email list, or developing a long-term partnership, business goals are often so daunting that doubt overtakes all focus and desire.

A foundational win is anything you've accomplished which you're also proud of, that you can mentally return to when goals become scary. By revisiting a previous personal victory, you remind yourself that you've already overcome difficult challenges. Think back to what you did at that time. Did you steel your mind and roll up your sleeves? Get specific about what you truly wanted? Break actions down into smaller pieces? Whatever approach you engaged in, consider how it worked, and how your challenge today compares. When your action has been clarified, step forward and win today's battle.

Once you've completed all of this work, you'll have a precise, action-oriented framework off of which to succeed in your niche and gain new customers. Remember: success is not only about doing one thing, or even one "right thing." **It's about proper, habitual implementation of the *correct* actions.**

Discover more Brad books here: Brad Johnson Books

21

THE POWER OF VISION

BARBARA MILLER

This chapter covers twelve success points in hosting a nonprofit Christian event which went from the impossible to a dramatic success.

1.   Having a vision big enough that others want to be part of it and want to help you achieve it

If you think small, you will only have a small amount of success. Small things don't usually excite people. I have found that if your vision is big enough, people will get behind it and want to see it work. This is especially true if it is a worthy cause or they see value in it. Not only that, people will want to help you make it work, so they can see your success as their success.

One example of this is when we went to the All Pacific Prayer Assembly (APPA) in New Zealand in 2005. The leaders said excitedly, "Here come the Millers!"

We were a little late arriving from Australia and a large group of people from all around the Pacific were already gathered. We wondered why everyone was excited about us, as this was our first time to meet with them.

It turned out that the leaders of the Pacific nations present, including the government and church leaders, had decided we should host the next yearly APPA conference in our city of Cairns, Australia. We were a bit overwhelmed to be greeted with this expectation. However, we decided to take up the challenge—but not without confirming prayer.

At the end of the conference, there was a big ceremony. The leaders handed over to us a canoe and the responsibility to organise the next conference. Why a canoe? The person who was the vision carrier and respected leader of the APPA was Rev Michael Maeliau from the Solomon Islands. He was also a member of parliament. He had a vision called the Deep Sea Canoe Vision where there would be a move of God's glory, like a large wave or cloud from the ends of the earth (the Pacific), back to Jerusalem. The glory cloud from Jerusalem would then cover the earth as the waters cover the sea, bringing forth revival before the end of the age. This vision was inspiring and empowering Christians in the Pacific Islands to get behind Michael, his second in charge, Pastor Milo Siilata, and the APPA.

2. Having faith in God and in yourself

But why my husband Norman and me? After all, there were already a couple of leaders from Australia—one from Brisbane and one from Sydney—who had been tracking with the group. Well, we were known for successfully running a number of Christian conferences in capital cities around Australia. Also, my husband is Aboriginal and they were keen to have an Indigenous leader host the conference to bring an Indigenous Australian flavour to it.

Another key reason was that we had just been appointed as the leaders for Australia of an international ministry called the Jerusalem House of Prayer for All Nations (JHOPFAN), a Christian organisation based in Jerusalem. We were also the appointed leaders of the Bethany Gate.

Pastor Tom Hess of JHOPFAN had a vision where he divided the world into twelve gates as a prayer strategy and appointed leaders for the twelve gates. Australia and part of Asia Pacific were in the Bethany Gate. The current leaders, Pastors Noel and Diane Mann, had just passed the leadership mantle to us. We were told in NZ that the conference was to be co-hosted by the APPA and the JHOPFAN. It became the Bethany Gate All-Pacific Prayer Assembly.

The conference in Australia was timed before and after May 14, 2006, the 400th anniversary of the explorer Pedro Ferdinand de Quiros's declaration. He landed on Vanuatu thinking he had discovered the elusive great southland (later called "Australia"). He took possession of the lands south of Vanuatu for the King of Spain and the Catholic church, declaring them the South Lands of the Holy Spirit. This declaration is held dear by many Christians in Australia and the Pacific as being prophetic over our region. It was to be a historic time. A number of visions were inspiring people at the same time.

Despite this, I don't think we could have taken on such an undertaking without faith in God and the experience that God had come through for us, as we had hosted conferences in the past by faith and without the money up front.

But were we up to this big a challenge?

3. Being brave enough to start a venture with no money

For a start, the organisations we had founded—the Centre for International Reconciliation and Peace and Tabernacle of David— had very little in the bank, and we were told the finances were our responsibility. How would we pay for it? Especially when the Pacific Islanders were used to being accommodated and fed three meals a day while at the conference for a nominal fee and it was to be a ten-day event. Hundreds were expected to attend.

4.   Having a vision to sustain you through the challenges and uncertainties

I prayed again when we got home, asking God if we were really meant to do it. I received more than one vision from the Lord about it, but this one resonated with us deeply. I recorded it:

"The second vision is about the canoe given in New Zealand to Norman and me to host the conference next year (in a baton hand-ing-on ceremony) which we brought back to Cairns. The canoe was beached on rocks but the Lord said that was okay, it has simply come to rest here. It then changed to the Ark of the Covenant and the Lord was saying to me, 'Don't let it go into the home of Obed Edom. It is meant to be a blessing to your house.' I believed the Lord was saying, 'This is a mantle for you and your ministry; don't give it away, keep it; it's going to be a blessing to you.' The Ark of the Covenant represents God's Glory."

Not leaving it in the home of Obed Edom was a reference to the time when King David of Israel wanted to bring the Ark of the Covenant, representing God's presence, into Jerusalem. It was brought in the wrong way, on a cart drawn by oxen, resulting in the death of one of the handlers. Upset, David left the ark in the home of Obed Edom. Months later, he received reports that Obed Edom had been blessed since he had housed the ark. So, David brought the ark to Jerusalem in the prescribed manner, dancing with joy that he could do so. I felt the Lord was telling me that hosting this conference was meant to bless me. He was saying, "Don't miss this opportunity by leaving it to another. You are meant to do it."

5.   Taking steps toward your dream and letting the universe fall in behind you

Fortified by this, we took on this enormous task. When we got the word out to Christians in Australia about us hosting this conference, a few donations started to come in. We had not asked for them, but people realized what a huge undertaking it would be. One friend in

Sydney sent us the largest donation, twenty thousand dollars. We used this to help hire a large marquis and chairs. We decided to hire the Cairns Showgrounds and put up a huge marquis, as we didn't have sufficient funds to hire any large conference rooms in a hotel. A large tent was a more appropriate setting anyway, and it meant we could afford to feed people on location, where we couldn't provide them with hotel lunches. This fit in with the name of our local congregation—Tabernacle (tent of David). We put the speakers and leaders of nations in hotels and paid for all their hotel meals.

6.   Being brave enough to risk failure

Registrations from around Australia helped too. We kept this at a reasonable rate, but it was higher than the nominal rate for the Pacific Islanders coming in. The APPA conference in New Zealand the previous year had about four hundred attendees, but we had over six hundred coming from PNG alone. I had to ring the airline and ask them to put on extra flights. How were we going to accommodate them?

We hired some extra marquis to put up at the showgrounds for accommodation. It became a tent city. What about beds? There had been a cyclone which had hit the town of Innisfail, just over an hour's drive away, worse than it had hit Cairns. They had a large number of mattresses they had used when people took refuge in a number of halls. The mattresses were no longer needed, and we were able to get them for free. We just had to pick them up.

However, the event was becoming bigger than Ben Hur, as the expression goes—and we had to take a deep breath and be prepared to risk failure. We had never done anything this big before and we couldn't afford any professional conference organisers to help us.

7.   Not giving up; finding a way when there is no way evident

Despite the challenges, we couldn't give up. We had to find a way. How would we feed people? We ran a number of concerts in Cairns and asked for donations of food or money, and this helped. Some people brought boxes of cereal. It also helped get the word out locally. There were a number of churches in Cairns with Pacific Islander pastors who were excited about the prospect of hosting their overseas Pacific family and helped out by cooking food during the conference. One church had some unused accommodation across the road from our home and they were able to house some of the overseas delegation for free. We paid for hostel accommodation for others. A church in Mareeba, over an hour away, let us use a medium-sized tent, which we used to serve food out of.

8. Working with like-minded people in unity so they are invested in the process and outcome instead of trying to own it yourself and do it all yourself

We had volunteers come into our church office and help with administration. We didn't ask them. They just turned up. One woman moved from Sydney to Cairns for six months to help us with administration. Another woman from the Atherton Tableland, an hour and a half away by car, came occasionally to help. Another from a local Cairns church came occasionally to help as well. As we had only one full-time administration worker and one occasional worker, this was a great help. They were both voluntary. I oversaw all the administration. It was a huge task. I had to write visa letters for over one thousand people. We even had people from Africa who wanted to come, but unfortunately the Australian government did not approve their entry.

9. Doing the hard yards and investing your time in what you believe you need to do

We put a lot of time into working with the Cairns Ministers Fraternal and local churches, involving those interested in regular planning meetings. This gave us a lot of support on the ground. We also paid for a one-page advertisement in our local newspaper so this gave us a good local attendance to our conference.

Inspired by George Otis Jr.'s transformation videos of city churches getting together in stadiums or showgrounds and having concerts in unity, it had been our desire for some time to see that happen in Cairns. So, we took the opportunity of our conference to give over the first night to the Cairns Ministers Fraternal. This was at considerable financial cost to us, but we let them run the first night and keep the offering—though they later gave us some of it. We had well over 2,500 people there from around the world – Israel, the Middle East, Asia, Australia, New Zealand, and almost every Pacific Island.

Somehow, we paid for the airfares, hotel accommodation, and meals of speakers to come in from Israel, Kuwait, India, Singapore, and the leaders from the Pacific. Somehow, we managed to pick up all the people from PNG who flew in, as Cairns is in the far north of Australia so it was reasonably accessible for them. A few days before the conference started, we would keep getting phone calls from the airport of people arriving from PNG who had not given us their arrival time. For those who had informed us, Norman was there with his van to pick them up. But for those arriving unannounced, he had to do a lot of trips back and forth to the airport to pick them up and try to find a place for them to stay. He took most of them to the Show-grounds. We had to accommodate and feed some people up to a week before the conference started and then up to a week afterwards. We put early arrivals from PNG and other nations up in hostels.

We had to hire a lot of sound equipment and lighting and set up a stage. During the conference, we did have significant outpours of rain and we are very thankful it didn't affect our equipment, cause safety issues, or dampen our spirits.

As there were going to be Prime Ministers and government leaders coming in from the Pacific nations, we felt we should organise a special breakfast for them with Australian Members of Parliament. This was an amazing time with wonderful speeches from MPs from the Pacific and Australia. Our international speakers attended too and, somehow, we picked up the tab.

We hired buses to ferry delegates around during the conference, and one church loaned us a minibus to help get people back to the airport afterwards. One day, we hired about twenty buses carrying fifty people each to go to an Aboriginal community about an hour's drive away. Many cars and vans accompanied us. Yarrabah is one of the largest Aboriginal communities in Australia and we have had a close working relationship with them for a long time. We asked them if they could put on a traditional feast of turtle, dugong, and other treats. At a reasonable cost to us, they put on a wonderful feast and traditional dancing in the park beside the Anglican church. It was a church by the sea and the atmosphere was electric with speeches, messages, and a wonderful exchange of cultures.

We even had a parade of the nations through the city with delegates wearing the traditional colourful costumes of their nations. We waved the flags of the nations and Christian banners during the parade.

The Pacific leaders wanted to put out a book for the event and I wrote one of the chapters for it. The conference sessions were videoed and we sold the DVDs during the conference, which helped us pay the costs.

10. Working with integrity and sticking to good values

Amazingly, we were able to donate six thousand dollars in cash to the PNG leaders to set up the Tabernacle of David and host the APPA event the following year. We donated seven thousand dollars by bank transfer to JHOPFAN for their work in Israel. We were also able to bless the speakers with good speaker donations. All this happened, though we had nothing to start with. Also, our co-hosts of APPA and JHOPFAN had provided no finances to enable us to host it. We took the financial gamble, we did the work, and everyone was blessed.

11. Co-hosting and/or networking with other organisations who have a following

However, if it had not been for the APPA, we would not have had the Pacific attendance we did, as they notified their large email list. Pastor Milo Siilata from NZ came to Cairns beforehand, visited the local churches, and encouraged them to participate. So, in large part, the success of the conference was due to the APPA following. The speakers we brought in from Asia, Israel, and the Middle East were leaders of JHOPFAN, so they were used to working together. Also, JHOPFAN advertised the event.

12. Providing a platform for others and honouring their gifts and callings

We had the most amazing speakers, topics, and panels with a mixture of overseas and local speakers. It was an enormous buzz of excitement, exchange of ideas, and spiritual inspiration.

Days were set aside for the Pacific leaders to run their yearly Men's Arise, Women's Arise, and Youth Arise meetings. As the largest group were women, they stayed at the Showgrounds and ran their meeting while we provided transport for the men to our Tabernacle of David church, which could hold about five hundred people. It had an Upper Room and those who were keen to pray prayed there 24/7 (taking turns) during the whole conference. This was the engine room, and the PNG people in particular were excited to go back to PNG after seeing how the Tabernacle of David worked, ready to set up their own. We hired another venue for the youth and it was wonderful to see all generations so engaged.

Was it a success?

Yes. Outstandingly successful, in many ways!

    1. **Good numbers.** Our administration staff at the conference

got overwhelmed and couldn't register all who turned up onsite. While we don't have exact numbers, we know there would have been over 2,500 people who attended during the day and more at night when it was free. Some estimates are up to four to five thousand people, because people came and went over the ten days.

2. **Spiritual Issues.** Very important spiritual issues were dealt with. Reconciliation occurred between Australia and those Pacific nations from which we kidnapped workers in the past to work on the sugar plantations of Queensland, our home state.

3. **Lives Changed.** Some peoples' lives changed forever with physical, spiritual, and emotional healing, as well as the new friendships made.

4. **Cultural Exchange.** The various nations enjoyed doing presentations of song and dance in their traditional dress and local languages. It was a wonderful time of cultural exchange.

5. **Visions Shared.** The visions of the APPA, JHOPFAN, and our Centre for International Reconciliation and Peace were shared and got a wider audience.

6. **Closer Ties.** Closer ties were forged between Australia, Asia, and Pacific nations.

7. **Bills paid and surplus.** We were able to pay our bills and bless other nations and ministries

You too can have success! Try it. Follow the principles above and follow your dreams and visions. This happened to be a Christian conference, but the success principles above can be applied to any situation.

So, what does it take? Vision is powerful! It needs to be big enough that others want to be part of it, and it needs to resonate with you so it can sustain you through difficulties. Having faith in God and faith in yourself is a key, as is being prepared to risk failure. As you step out bravely toward your dream, you help to make it real. Others will step in to help you. It is important not to give up, but to do the hard yards and invest your time and energy. Work with good values and show integrity. Partnering and networking with others who have a following or who simply want to work with you in unity is important. Be prepared to give others a platform. Support them and honour them, and you will find it will come back to you. In the end, we are not in it for what we can get out of it, but for what we can do for others. This is a recipe for success.

More books from Barbara Miller: Barbara Miller Books

22

IN SYNC: THE KEY TO MAGNETIC SALES, BONDING CUSTOMER SERVICE, AND TRANSFORMATIVE LEARNING PROGRAMS

ROY VARNER

Every interaction with another human being – in person, by Zoom, via ads, or elsewhere – is a chance to help that individual enjoy a better self-image.

What better life purpose than to bless everyone with whom we come in contact...lift spirits...share ideas that ease pains...lessen fears...stimulate "AHA!" moments! Help one another through real coaching to get unstuck and nudge ourselves to a higher mindset, to thrive emotionally and financially. Maybe just feel a bit better about how today is going.

This other-directed life purpose led me to a career of developing learning systems to "teach people how to fish": to empower them with key information, skills, and best practices to be independent and self-sufficient in meeting their life's needs and wants. I wanted to be the hero who enabled each one to make a huge leap in self-confidence and flourish.

Facilitating lasting change of people's minds and behavior like Johnny Appleseed, however, turned out to be a whole lot more like painfully slogging ever so slowly through a quagmire of quicksand.

My own experience across four decades of developing learning systems and video/film programs to "train" many thousands of employees at major corporations finally honed and clarified my universal toolbox of "street-smart" techniques that consistently got lasting results. There was no mistaking the empirical confirmations that the "magical" process to empower humans to change is actually a universal formula based on how the human mind works, not on demographics.

Understanding humans' tremendous resistance to change – and the critical process needed to guide them out of that self-imposed prison -- has been perhaps the one most important factor in any successes I have had in business and life.

IN SYNCH: Drawn Together by Resonation, the Law of Attraction

I think of magical mindset **being mentally IN SYNC**, like a team of synchronized swimming *(or getting a Vulcan mind meld for us baby boomers)*. Resonating with how another sees things. Feeling like-minded, as kindred spirits. On the same frequency, drawn together by the Law of Attraction. *"Wow, you really understand me!"*

Let me share some "AHA!" moments from research on how the human mind works, and then I'll wrap with ways to make sure your business is always IN SYNC with your customers for major growth and long-term momentum.

We must start by understanding that the human mind, or psyche, has been programmed from early man's more dangerous times to be an entrenched, jealous bodyguard sworn to defend its person from trauma *(physical and mental)*. This psyche does so by circling the wagons around a self-defined *safety zone*. Each defensive psyche adopts a **set of limiting assumptions** as a result of emotional life experiences, especially from what critical family members and friends declare about one's obvious shortcomings along the way. These self-accepted tenets are emotion-based core beliefs about one's self-worth and expectations of how the world behaves: *I'm not good* *enough to compete...can't handle tech stuff...terrified of public speaking because I will surely screw up and look like a stupid idiot...I deserved the beating my husband gave me...and so on.*

Defensive Coping Behaviors Become Limiting Daily Habits

Then the mind creates its royal guard of *coping behaviors* to protect those limiting assumptions in one's safety zone from scary invasion or extraction. Think of the inertial rest state of doing nothing *(common response to overwhelm)*...procrastination *(often fear of failure)*... hiding from the spotlight...fibbing to appear better or smarter than we are...setting rigid relationship boundaries...and so on).

These defensive behaviors become ingrained daily habits that tunnel our vision and keep us from learning and growing to higher mindsets. Fear-based habits keep us from writing that new book or actually finishing most any project or task. They are behind why we take courses and never finish them, drop out of college, give up too soon in our businesses, and bail from struggling relationships. Trying to change them can create aggression *(fight)* or emotional withdrawal and entrenchment *(flight)*.

Short story...years ago a major corporation was suffering high turnover of employees and customers, even though its annual customer survey *(the "How are we doing?" postcard)* always showed at least 95% customer satisfaction *(asking the wrong questions always gives false positives)*. My company was hired to develop a program to train their workers to be nicer to customers, so managers could sleep at night and the legal department could C the company's A. Weeks of interviews with management, employees, and customers revealed that employees were seeing things only through their own perspective of stressful daily run-ins with gnarly customers, who likewise had their own POV of heartless corporate workers. As always, management cranked up the pressure through quotas and unrealistic deadlines, and predictably, frustrated employees chose flight and went elsewhere.

What eventually worked was a custom, coached program called

"Handle With Special C.A.R.E." *(Concern, Assurance, Responsiveness, and Excellence).* Week one focused solely on putting employees in their customers' shoes through the immersion of being the customer. They had to turn off their "employee" mindset and see the company's services, failures, rules, etc. as though they were the customers receiving the treatment. From then on, as if by magic, they began to resonate with customer complaints and pains instead of their former knee-jerk defensive reactions to them. These enlightened individuals embraced the role of *customer ombudsman* within company P&P rules. The attitude turnaround was contagious and changed the culture in all company locations that supported the program. The metrics began to correct as well.

Another quick story...truck drivers on a tight schedule to pick up residential garbage were constantly turning corners too quickly, leaving deep ruts in peoples' lawns or landscaping. The driver's supervisor had to take a truck out to the site and repair the damage under a barrage of profanity from the furious customer. The solution was for drivers to experience the same point-of-view exercise until they realized they needed to think like customers and care about their needs. We created a sign on a stake to put in a yard whenever a driver made a rut, showing his/her name and saying, *"Sorry! I will be back by (time later that day) to fix this!"* Then the driver had to return at the end of a long, tiring shift to personally make it right. Soon the rut reports ceased completely, replaced by "thank you" calls from customers who found drivers and crew to be friendly, courteous, and understanding about their needs.

What do these two stories have in common?

A Mindset IN SYNC With Customers' Needs and Best Interests

In each case, individuals needed to get drop their old, limiting assumptions and related unproductive coping behaviors and get IN SYNC with their customers' needs and best interests. It took a week of seeing life from the customer's point of view and vicariously experiencing the pains, fears, needs and wants of those they were being paid to serve, to truly change their ways. With that understanding and empathy, they recognized unproductive thinking *(negative assumptions)* and coping behavior *(behavioral habits)* that had to change – and they willingly embraced a better way to think and act in resonance with their customers.

This learning process made it easy for them to give themselves permission to abandon the old and embrace the new, because they understood the difference now and truly wanted to be better. As a result, they began to work outside the lines of previous emotional safety zones, one step at a time, as their self-confidence and expectation for good increased over time.

Now, understand that this process is not self-improvement, which for most people doesn't work as a way to change lives. In fact, **97% of people really can't recognize or give up their programmed, limiting assumptions on their own without a coach or mentor,** especially if the assumptions came from real childhood trauma. Humans make decisions emotionally and then justify them logically with their coping and rationalizing behavior. Expecting people to change their emotional cores and defense systems by passively receiving information and hearing rah-rah pep talks *(neither of which is enough to cause change)* is why **97% of people who pay thousands for online programs never finish them nor get the promised leap of mindset to a thriving level.** Typically, those long, talking-face videos and core dumps of information overwhelm us *("I can't deal with all this!"),* so we choose the lesser pain of quitting and returning to old, comfortable ways.

The proven way to get a person to change and adopt higher mindsets is through the true *1:1 coaching process:* Identify limiting assumptions and expose why they aren't working for the individual... show a better way, focusing on one skill or process...let the person practice applying the new way, with the coach's positive and constructive feedback...assign practice away from the coach...rejoin and review what worked, what didn't...reaffirm the best practice...have the person explain the new way to another *(we get serious clarity when preparing to explain it to others)*...have the person verbally commit to embrace and adopt the new way...and follow up later to ensure there's no backsliding.

1:1 Coaching Process Grows Self-Confidence to Move Ahead

The greatest benefit of this change process is not the new knowledge *(how-to books may inspire but seldom result in mindset leaps)*, but rather the **bump in self-confidence** that each such experience gives the learner. A building-block sequence of learning experiences, each around one skill or practice, lets the learner gain momentum and get that big jump in self-confidence that empowers new and braver thinking and behavior.

Who is going to change the world: a rote memorizer of data, or a confident, make-it-happen person who believes he or she can accomplish any task or goal?

That's a mindset leap. That's change. That's transformation from reluctant victim to a conscious system of can-do self belief. *There's no more important transformation for an individual than strong growth in self-confidence...the key to the prison door.*

Three Major Ways Being IN SYNC Can Turbocharge Your Business

Now I promised to show how to apply this IN SYNC magic to make your business grow and thrive, and help your customers do the same. Here are highlights of three of my coaching programs, in a nutshell.

Being IN SYNC is the key to creating *highly-converting sales videos and online ads* that draw prospects to your solutions:

1. **Grab attention** by leading with your ideal prospect's major pain, fear, or need so you can attract his/her attention to stop surfing and look at your message *(the relevance than answers the question, "What's in it for me?")*;
2. **Heighten visceral memory of emotional feelings** about

the problem by quickly listing a few most common scenarios in your customers' lives;

3. **Offer hope of solution** based on your experience and authority, supported by social proof of transformations; and

4. **Call for action** to "click here" to investigate this hopeful solution. Do all of that with their own words they used to explain their pains, fears, needs, and wants in your surveys.

Being IN SYNC is also key to *maintaining a warm and valued relationship with your customers over time.* Critical steps include sending regular, valuable information aimed at what you know they need and want *(no selling)*...talking about them in their own words and sharing their stories...responding quickly and supportively to all inquiries and problems...and giving such exceptional, personal service *(always adding value)* that they wouldn't think of going anywhere but to their IN-SYNC resource.

Being IN SYNC is also key to *creating and managing online coaching and information programs:*

1. **Create your program's transformation promise** *(desired outcome)* based on your prospects' key words to describe their greatest pain, fear, or need *(making sure you're committed to deliver that promise for all students);*

2. **Identify 5-7 learning objectives** *(mini-transformations)* that sequentially achieved will build up to achieving the major program transformation;

3. **For each learning objective, list 3-5 tasks** a person needs to be able to do and feel good about in order to achieve that particular objective; and

4. **For each task, choose a highly engaging activity** that will best help the learner master it before moving on to the next task or learning objective.

THE NET OF BEING FULLY IN SYNC

In summary, being fully IN SYNC with your ideal customers is the one critical mental and emotional connection that makes them feel you are a kindred spirit who understands them. You then become their ideal solution, that valuable resource with the "all clear" resonance that lets them lower their safe-zone defenses and choose to change.

Get and stay IN SYNC in all your business communications and you will discover the three "golden" benefits of that magical mindset: *high conversion rates and sales...high transformation rates for students of your coaching/learning programs...and high retention rates for your growing family of raving customer fans!*

Now, the ball's in your court. Are you ready to make IN SYNC magic work for your business and every customer?

Need help getting in sync for higher conversions, transformations, and tribe retention?

Schedule a free session with Transformation Coach Roy Varner at RoyVarner.com

23

CODE YOUR MIND FOR SUCCESS

STEPHEN PARR

Early days

It wasn't that I hated school. I just struggled to pass exams. I knew the subject matter but my brain seemed to seize up on me, or my memory failed. I still remember the time when, in the final exams, only a few weeks before I was done with school forever, I received my worst mark ever: 35% Ouch. How did that happen? It was just as well that I had already been accepted into my chosen career, but I remained very upset. I eventually decided to sit the exam again the following year and study for it by remote learning.

About that time I was blessed with a stroke of luck. I was an avid reader and spent a lot of time roaming the bookshelves in our local library. On one occasion, I found myself picking out a book—or did it pick me?—called *Self-Hypnotism* by L. M. LeCron. It offered such gems as memory improvement, overcoming anxiety, and achieving goals. That book changed my life. When I re-sat the exam the next year, I achieved my highest mark ever.

Since then, I have read most of the classic mind development books and explored various mind development systems. Along the way, I became proficient and qualified in Clinical Hypnotherapy, Neurolinguistic Programming (NLP), and meditation practice.

Now, let us turn to your future and explore a range of well-proven thought and mind-management techniques to enable you to achieve your goals even as you sleep.

The Mind: Conscious and Subconscious

We need to first consider the mind, which is an immensely complex subject. We are going for the very simple version. The mind is sometimes compared to an iceberg, in that our conscious mind is similar to that part of the iceberg that is visible and above water, while our subconscious is likened to that greater part of the iceberg that is hidden below the water.

Our conscious mind is our wakeful awareness at any point in time. It is what we use in our daily activities to read, speak, reason, make conclusions, and make decisions. We use it to initiate and carry out complex activities, such as driving and playing sports. At night, we give it a rest when we sleep.

The subconscious, however, is at work constantly. It controls the mechanisms of our body, such as breathing. It also stores everything which is not in our conscious mind. This includes all of our present and past memories, beliefs, feelings, and experiences—both positive and negative. These form self-belief patterns that our subconscious uses to influence our behaviors and guide our outer life experiences to conform to. It is possible to re-code some of these self-belief patterns, and thus change our outer experiences.

The Code

A Success Code is similar to the lines of code in a computer program. Code instructs a computer what to do at any point in time. We live in an age of information. Technology, computers, and modern mobile phones are our tools. What about our own internal computer—the mind? How important is it to program that for success? Take a look at the following quotes and decide for yourself.

For as he thinketh in his heart, so is he...

— (PROVERBS 23:7)

We are what we think we are.

— SOCRATES

We are what we think. All that we are arises with our thoughts. With our thoughts we make the world.

— BUDDHA

A man is but the product of his thoughts; what he thinks, he becomes.

— MAHATMA GANDHI

Think and Grow Rich.

— NAPOLEON HILL (THE FATHER OF SUCCESS)

Whatever the mind can conceive and believe, it can achieve.

— NAPOLEON HILL

These quotes from some of the great minds of the world. They clearly confirm that success comes from the mind, and so that is the focus of this chapter. *We are what we think we are,* so we need to become more aware of our thoughts. We need to re-code, or reprogram, our minds for success.

Mind Gardens

Think of your subconscious mind as a garden where thoughts are seeds that grow into plants. These plants may be either beneficial or weeds. Regularly spend time tending your mind garden so as to weed out unwanted or harmful thoughts and memories. Replace them with desirable thoughts and memories. This sounds easy, but it is easier said than done. Think how difficult it is to weed out an unhelpful habit or start a new one. Fortunately, there are numerous techniques and books that can help our mind gardening. Most of the techniques are useful on their own, but when used together the results can be amazing.

Books

A good place to start searching for books is *Amazon Kindle eBooks,* because they are low-cost and can be downloaded from almost anywhere in the world.

On the general subject of thinking, Edward de Bono is a leading global authority with over sixty books written on the subject. He developed new concepts including Lateral Thinking and Parallel Thinking. His instructions in thinking have been used in some of the leading corporations across the world, such as IBM, BT, Nokia, and Siemens. One of his books that I particularly enjoyed is called *How to Have a Beautiful Mind.* This also contains a section on his *Six Thinking Hats* concept.

A Calm Mind

Just the thought of having a calm mind will seem a wonderful achievement to some people. Start building your calm mind habit by simply sitting still for five or ten minutes with a gentle focus on your breath. Later you could choose another focus, such as a calming word, thought, mental image, or meditative music. To help establish this as a habit, you could use your car as a trigger, and spend a few minutes practicing your calm mind whenever you get into or out of your car.

Take your attention to your breath and feel each inflow and outflow. Even doing this on a regular basis for two to three minutes will be beneficial, and each time you do this you will generate an accumulative effect. Try it.

It may be a little difficult at first, particularly if you have a busy mind with a great many thoughts rattling around in it. Let the thoughts flow, but do not get caught up in them. If you do, just move your attention back to your chosen focus or to your breath as a focus. A little perseverance should result in you enjoying these short mind breaks and looking forward to them. This is a simple and very useful introduction to meditation.

Mindfulness

The practice of mindfulness presents an opportunity to both broaden and sharpen your mind, as well as to enrich your life experience. As a starting point, while sitting in your calm mind space gently become mindful of every external aspect of where you are—the sounds, the temperature, how you are feeling in your body. Then, move your attention to the flow of your thoughts. Just become an observer of the thoughts. Do not follow or engage. This is a unique opportunity to observe your own mind and reflect on what you observe. It may be useful to keep a journal of your observations because this may be where you discover some specific and persistent negative thoughts, feelings, or emotions. Then you have something to work with, using affirmations or NLP reframing techniques. A journal is a great way of observing and recording your developing mindset and how that changes over time as you engage in more Success Code mental practices.

You can extend the use of mindfulness into your day to day activity, including your relationships, home life, work life, and even driving. Your world will become richer as you fully observe it.

Affirmations and Positive Self Talk

Affirmations are nothing new. One of the most famous has been in use for about one hundred years. "Every day, in every way, I am getting better and better" was developed by French psychologist Emile Coué (1857-1926). He advocated repeating it many times while in a state of passive relaxation, such as just before going to sleep or upon waking. Passive relaxation is important, because the more you relax your mind the more access you have to your subconscious.

I suggest that you start with the Coué affirmation as your foundation, and then add more to suit your specific mindset goals. Keep them positive, in the present tense, and about yourself. Start off with simple things that are easily achievable, so your mind starts to build evidence that they are working. Use them with the intent and expectation that they will work. If you can identify some thoughts that are holding you back or even seem to be sabotaging your efforts, design an affirmation to reframe or counter this, so that it will lose energy and shrivel up like a weak weed. Construct affirmations that best describe a skill or state that you wish to experience, but in terms of you already being there. For example, "I am grateful that my income is now steadily increasing (or health is now steadily improving)." Finally, expect miracles.

Turbo boosting techniques

You can supercharge your affirmations by including Gratitude and Creative Visualization, as well as by Energizing them with your passion.

Gratitude is a shortcut to reprogramming the mind, and certainly to enhancing affirmations. Make a point each day of finding at least one thing you are grateful for and express it internally as an affirmation. Continue this practice diligently, and you will find that you spend more time in a positive mindset. Your subconscious mind will present you with more opportunities to be grateful for.

Creative Visualization is the technique of using your imagination to create what you want in life. This is a favored technique with sports people. They imagine and feel themselves achieving on the sports field in advance of the real thing. Start by getting into a relaxed state of mind, as this will enable you to access a more creative part of your brain. Then, decide on an idea, inspiration, or goal to use as the focus and allow or invite your subconscious mind to imagine or just think about yourself successfully in that situation. Imagine what you would be feeling, including being grateful for your success. Imagine yourself being congratulated by others. Imagine yourself being really passionate about reaching for and achieving your goal.

By using these techniques diligently, your subconscious mind will become like an unseen partner assisting you, even as you sleep, in your journey through a successful life.

May you be blessed with everlasting gratitude and share the fruits of your success with those in need.

Learn more at StephenParrBooks.com.

24

MANIFEST THE LIFE YOU WANT

MARIE TEMBY

When I was asked to be a co-author in this book I had to pinch myself. The offer was finally real. My dream for many years was to help others, and it has been coming to life every day. I managed to create a life of success not only in my eyes, but—more importantly— in the eyes of others.

Here is my story in a nutshell...

I grew up in a small country town, Broken Hill, in the outback of Australia. I was one of six siblings living in a three-bedroom house. My garage today is bigger than that whole house.

My mother was amazing at looking after us all—washing, ironing, food shopping, cooking, cleaning. I cannot remember her ever doing anything for herself. My father was a good father, but was unwell for many years, which I believe was the catalyst that led him to drink a lot. We were considered a poor family, but our home was full of love.

University wasn't something my parents could afford, so getting a higher education wasn't an option for me. I didn't have the same opportunities others had, so I had to make my own.

After school, I worked in a café, making milkshakes and sand-wiches until I had saved enough money to move to the city and attend business college.

Fast forward a few years and I've met my future husband at the young age of nineteen. By twenty-seven and twenty-eight we were holding a key to our first franchise. Within seven years we had a key to our second franchise, we married, had three children—tragically one did not survive. We were successfully living a full life.

Phew! That sounded so quick, writing that...although, looking back, it really did feel that quick.

Those years were overwhelming for me. I was out of control on the inside. To my friends and family, I looked like I had it all: a happy family, successful business, and lots of great holidays. It was true. I did have it all, only I lived with an overwhelming anxious feeling through many of those years.

Our business has been very successful and provided our family with many great things. There is a misconception out there about success, and that is luck. My experience has taught me "success comes from hard work." When you find it, you can take your foot off the pedal only for so long. To maintain success, you need to keep the engine going at some level.

Where my dream began to come to life...

In our first year in business, we went on a short holiday with eight other franchisees. During this trip, I discovered others were having the problems I thought were just ours. I decided at that moment I would document our experiences with one intention: to help people in the future who would be going down the same path. Two decades later, I have pages of notes—on anything I considered helpful, ideas that worked, ideas that didn't—dedicated toward making others' journeys not so overwhelming. I have them all in what I call my trea-sure chest. I had a burning passion to bring this all to life.

For many years, I had three goals on my vision board. I had completed two of them, so I had one left. It was starting to look like I was never going to make it come to life. This goal was to write my book.

The dream coming to life ...

Coming back from a trip with my youngest son in the car, I was listening to an audiobook. I asked him to listen, as well.

His reply stung a little, but it was just what I needed to hear. "Mum, when are you going to stop listening to other people's books and write yours?"

Their whole lives, my children watched me take notes for my book and heard me talk about it. I continually told them anything was possible and to chase their dreams. This was a moment where I thought, if I didn't make this happen for myself, why should they believe it to be true?

After this trip, I spent time trying to make it happen but I just couldn't. I asked my husband for permission to take some time away from our business to solely focus on my book. I desperately wanted to complete it, and I always thought it was the business holding me back.

He allowed me the time to do this and, to our surprise, writing about our journey and the business invigorated me and my involvement in the process. This is where I truly learned to follow your passion. Don't leave it behind—no regrets.

Some of our success tips...

Working together with your partner in business can be hard unless you set some rules. We did this from day one, and we have never broken them. Here are two of our best:

1. Never argue in front of our staff, no matter how tempting. We had to be united in their eyes.
2. We divided the store into sections, then decided who would be in charge of each section. If we ever disagreed on

how something should be done, the person in charge of that section had the final say.

Staff and Team Building: Staff are vitally important to your business. It is crucial to continually train them, listen to them, and provide them a safe workplace. If they feel loved, in return they will love your business. I have a free handbook for employers to give to their employees on my website: 7 tips to be extraordinary.

Team building: I have incorporated many team activities that involved bringing the staff together with a common goal. Each time, they have increased sales but also had fun in the stores.

Customers: I make sure our staff knows how important every single customer is who walks through our door. I don't want them to receive good or great customer service—I want them to experience extraordinary service. Fun fact: did you know that for every bad customer experience, the customer will share it with ten people? For every extraordinary experience, the customer will share with one. Food for thought.

Balance: I searched long and hard for this and can honestly say I have it. The biggest breakthrough for me was when I decided to look at our personal and professional life as one. By doing this I was never concerned one was stealing time from the other. I began adding more into my life. It really was that simple.

Rituals: I noticed a common thing that all the great and successful people in life have: Daily rituals. No one tells the story of rituals better than Hal Elrod in his book, *The Miracle Morning*. I slowly added rituals to my everyday life. I now have my own system which includes completing ten different rituals every single day of my life. If you would like a free download of these, visit my website: marietemby.com.

Gratitude: In 2018 I posted every single day on my personal Facebook page something I was grateful for. Not only did I notice many things I had to be grateful for which were always there, I also created extra things.

Paperwork: This would have to be the most tedious part of any business, and certainly one that gave me lots of stress over the years. I came up with a system for every piece of paperwork that came across my desk: delegate, defer, automate, or delete. I write about this in great detail in my book, *Simple Soulful Successful.*

The dream was born...

In 2019 I signed up with a publisher, Rob Kosberg, and went about writing my book *Simple Soulful Successful: A Mum-preneurs Journey To Daily Happiness, Through Business, Balance And Rituals.* It became a #1 International Bestseller in many categories on Amazon and I couldn't be prouder of the people the book has helped and the path it has taken me on.

If you write a bestselling book, it doesn't instantly make you successful. It is what you do with that book that makes the difference. If you are passionate about your topic, authentic in how you deliver the message, and truly believe you can help others, success *will* come your way. But you have to be patient. Anything worth having is worth waiting for. There is a lot of work that you need to do after you have the book, and Ray Brehm has been amazing at guiding me through all of that.

Ten of my life principles, I'm continually guided by...

- FAMILY FIRST – Strong and secure families don't just happen; you must put work into creating a bond that hopefully carries forward generations.
- PASSION – Not everyone knows what their passion is, but we all have one, so search deeply until you find it and then go for it.
- GRATITUDE – Have a journal next to your bed and write something to be grateful for every night. One day, you will look back over it and realize many things in life you have had to be grateful for.

- HEALTH – Include a form of exercise in your daily plan, even if it's just a short walk. Eat something you know is good for you.
- LEARNING – Keep learning. There is power in learning at any stage of life, especially if you are passionate about what it is you are learning.
- POSITIVITY – Limit any interaction with negativity and focus on the positive. I like to send positive messages to people I care about and read positive affirmations daily.
- RITUALS – Incorporate rituals into your life, and complete ten every day.
- IMPROVEMENT – Maintain a philosophy of continuous improvement in both your personal and professional life.
- HONESTY – If you live life with honesty and loyalty, you will die with dignity. Only make a promise when you know you can follow it through.
- SPIRITUALITY – Participate in some form of spirituality every day, like a meditation, mindfulness, or watching a sunset.

How it all fits together...

During my years, I have attended many conferences, listened to great speakers, purchased online courses, and attended masterminds.

I am a true believer that you can manifest the life you want and that we all have the power to control our thoughts. Dr. Joe Vitale has been pivotal in teaching me that you can have, do, or be whatever you want.

But you cannot do it alone. You must seek help at different stages of that path to teach yourself what is out there. That young girl in Broken Hill did not know how to run a business, how to be in charge of staff, or how to write a book, but she did have a passion to learn it all and become successful.

When you hold onto your beliefs, search for the answers, and don't let anyone tell you it isn't possible, the right people will turn up in your life. That is exactly what happened to me.

What is next…

Who knows exactly where I am going to end up? I do know that I will be happy wherever it is, because I am doing what I love and working on my passion.

Everything I teach comes from the heart. It is simple to understand, and it works. I'm not just saying it—I have experienced it working for myself.

I'm currently working on three online courses, each designed to help small business owners find daily happiness and be successful at the same time. The topics will be: "Steps To Make Your Staff Extraordinary," "Building A Great Team," and "Creating More Happiness And Balance."

I design my own planners, and for years I have been experimenting to find the perfect planner. Many were great, but I wanted one that had everything I needed, so I designed it.

I wish you the success you deserve, but if you take one tip from everything you have read, take this: don't wait for it. Go out and grab it.

You can reach Marie at www.marietemby.com or https://www. facebook.com/simplesoulfulsuccessful/.

25

FIGHT THE COBRA

MONICA RUBOMBORA

My mama has always been a fighter, but on this day, she was fighting for her life—as well as the lives of her brood of six children, who were all under ten years of age.

An enormous snake had just fallen out of a tree into our play area. My little brother spotted it first.

"Snake!" he screamed. We all froze.

"You all get up and run into the house, and lock the door now!" Mama screamed.

Once in the house, we scuttled to the window and peeped out to watch as a tug of war erupted between Mama and the snake.

The snake stood up, almost at eye-level, and looked menacingly at her. Mama grabbed a piece of firewood and hit at it until it fell down. Then, amazingly, the snake stood up again, and started moving towards her. She hit at it again, and it fell. It stood up again.

I don't recall how long this went on, but the snake eventually got down and started slithering toward the outdoor kitchen house. Mama ran towards it, all the while trying to hit at it with the piece of firewood. She did not want it to enter the kitchen house nor did she want it to go toward the main house, where we all were. The snake turned and slid under a bunch of firewood that was lying in the yard. Mama pulled the bunch of firewood apart.

The battle ended when the snake slipped out from under the bunch of firewood and disappeared into the tall grass.

We later learned that the snake was a king cobra, one of the most venomous snakes in Africa.

Success is an Obligation

Success is my obligation. It is a pact I have signed with myself. The expectation is that I should honour it.

Success is vital for my survival, the survival of my family, and the survival of the community I live in. It is my responsibility to become successful so I can take good care of myself and the people I care about. There is so much that is at stake here. I have got to wake up prepared to fight for it every day. Lives depend on it.

The desire to succeed is like a fire that's constantly burning deep within my gut. It drives me. It spurs me into action every day.

It is this sense of duty that helps to keep me focused on pursuing success, and I am committed to making it happen.

It is the right thing to do.

"May he give you the desire of your heart and make all your plans succeed."

— PSALM 20:4

Success is About Being Known for Something

I know that the work I do has inspired and touched many people. I want to do more of that. I want to do so on a grander scale so I can inspire many more people to succeed. I want to put myself and the work I do out into the world. I want to leave meaningful footprints everywhere, footprints that will outlive me. This is the reason I write books. This is the reason I speak on many public platforms. This is the reason I coach, mentor, and train people. I want to bloom wherever I am planted.

"Oh, that you would bless me and enlarge my territory!"

— *1 Chronicles 4:10*

Success is About Being Present

Being present is a practice that has served me well over the years. If I don't show up in front of my clients, if I don't listen to what is keeping them awake at night, if I don't present myself as someone they can trust to solve their problems, then I won't be successful in winning their business.

You cannot catch opportunities when you are absent. Success is about being present. You need to show up and immerse yourself into being of help to others. Then, somehow, luck will keep coming your way. Be prepared to grab the opportunity that will present itself.

One of the most important contracts of my career came about because I was in the right place at the right time, with key decision makers in the room. I had gone into the boardroom on a different matter—to deliver a progress report about another unrelated project. A few weeks later, I got an additional project contract because a potential client in that boardroom believed that I was the most suitable person to do the work. I got put in charge of the entire business portfolio.

"Do you not know that in a race all the runners run, but only one gets the prize? Run in such a way as to get the prize."

— *1 Corinthians 9:24*

Success is About Using Fear As a Motivator

As far back as I can remember, I always dreamt of writing a best-selling book. I had a lot of book ideas and book titles. I wrote every day; I still do. I would file away each incomplete manuscript, never letting them see the light of day.

I later moved into a management and technology consulting business. There is a lot of writing involved in this kind of work. My work colleagues soon nicknamed me the "Proposal Queen." They told me I wrote great client proposals. I was the go-to person each time a proposal writing requirement came up.

I also write customer reviews for other products and services. I get sent "free" stuff to experience and then write reviews about them. I also write book reviews for other authors. I post one or two book reviews a week. I even have a badge on Amazon, the world's biggest marketplace, signifying me as one of their top book reviewers.

Even with these writing accolades, I still nurtured a dream of writing and publishing a book—like the ones I was writing reviews for. But I could never bring myself to doing so.

Over the years, I accumulated a collection of books about "How to write a book," and "How to be a writer," and "How to write and publish a book." I even enrolled myself into writing clubs. I cheered on and celebrated with one person after the other as they wrote and published their books. I could not get over my self-doubt.

Fear held me back. The fear was not about the book, as I knew I could write. My fear was that people would discover that I have written a book and then *read* the book! Disaster! What if they hated it? Would they think I am fraud? And how would I handle the negative feedback?

Fear is a debilitating emotion. It is a confidence killer. A barrier to success. It keeps you immobilized in one spot as time rushes by.

That was true, until I learned how to use fear as a signal to fight back. Then fear spurred me into action. The more action I put in, the more the fear subsided.

I concluded that it is what you do with fear that matters. I could use fear as a force for good. Fear can be tackled head-on. Once confronted, it dissipates.

"... Be strong, fear not..."

— ISAIAH 35:4

The Euphoria of Accomplishment

There is something magical about taking on a challenge and then succeeding. One gets a thrill out of the chase and an even bigger thrill once one lands the deal. Success gets addictive. You want more. You want to do it again. Success begets more success.

After many years of attempting to write a book, I eventually got around to writing and publishing one. I recall hitting the "PUBLISH" button one late night and going to bed. I woke up the next morning to find the coveted orange "Best Seller" banner on my book. The book became a Number One best-seller in all its listed Amazon categories overnight. I followed that up with two physical book launches and the events were both sold out. To say that I was euphoric would be an understatement.

The momentum has continued. I have since written and published more books, and I am also coaching aspiring writers to do the same.

Becoming a published author has also added credibility to the other work I do. It has opened more doors for me as a sought-after coach, mentor, trainer, and public speaker.

"... the Lord instructed Moses, "Write this down on a scroll as a permanent reminder..."

— EXODUS 17:14

Success is About What You Spend Time On

You are what you spend your time on. You become successful at whatever you invest your time in. Once you commit to doing something, put in the hours.

I believe that I have succeeded not because I am the smartest person in the room, but because I work hard. I succeed because once I commit to doing something, I put in the hours. I work until it gets done. Time gets blurred as I become consumed with the tasks at hand. The more time I put into something, the more successful I become. I do whatever it takes to get it done. I become obsessed with doing it until I succeed.

> *"You shall eat the fruit of the labor of your hands; you shall be blessed, and it shall be well with you."*
>
> — PSALM 128:2

Success is About Habits

Success is a verb. We should not leave it to chance. It needs to reflect in my everyday habits.

If you become what you do every day, then it makes sense to work at being successful every single day. I have to work on developing the right habits that will keep my head in the right mind-space.

As I write this chapter, South Africa is going through the COVID-19 virus health crisis lockdown. The crisis has caused one of the biggest disruptions of our time. It is chaotic out there, and it appears like life will never be normal again.

Huddled inside my house, I found sanity in sticking to some old habits, structure, and routine in my daily schedules. The only difference was that the bulk of the tasks are being done indoors.

For example, there are some consistent things I do during the first two to three hours of each waking day. On a typical morning, after the normal morning chores, I sit at my desk, and the first act is to switch off the phone, disable the WiFi, and set a timer for thirty minutes. Then I write. I write every day—even on Christmas Day. I also work in thirty-minute bursts, as that seems to be the length of my concentration span.

I pull out a notebook and write my goals. I write my goals down every single day. Usually, they are the same goals that I would have written three months earlier. Working daily towards these self-imposed goals is critical to my success.

I switch off my phone again and do some deep-brain work for another hour or two. This mainly involves working on content for client proposals and client deliverables.

Then I hit the phone and make calls to existing and prospective clients or partners. I set aside time to make these calls and send text messages. I make a lot of calls, and I send a lot of messages. It is intentional; if I didn't make these calls, the work pipeline would quickly dry up.

I dedicate most afternoons to overseeing and coordinating my various teams' progress on various contracted projects. I also keep in touch with my clients to make sure they are happy with our performance. Then I spend the rest of the afternoon doing paperwork and other administrative tasks.

The early evenings are for family time. I prepare dinner on most nights while chatting to my husband, who usually works on his patients' files at the kitchen table. Cooking is one of the few things that really shifts me into a different mental state.

I then get back to my desk at about 10 p.m. and get into a webinar, write, or read until around midnight. On those days when a client deadline is looming, I go to bed when I see the sky brightening so that "tomorrow doesn't catch me looking into yesterday!"

It is a routine that has stayed fairly constant over the years, and that provided comfort, structure, and sanity during the global COVID-19 health crisis.

"But as for you, be strong and do not give up, for your work will be rewarded."

— 2 CHRONICLES 15:7

Success is About Meaningful Relationships

The work that I do requires significant outside help. The teams I work with are far smarter than me (without them, I would be toast!). I am who I am because of others, and I know that I can only be as successful as the people I surround myself with. When the teams hit their goals, I hit mine tenfold.

Working with teams also helps me to stay accountable to them and to myself. Once I announce to one or more of the team members that we will pursue and close a deal or that I will create great content, I subconsciously feel an obligation to live up to the promise. For example, had it not been for an accountability partner, I would not have gotten my first book completed and published.

Success means that I can offload some work and afford to pay other people to do so as well whilst I concentrate on my creative side.

Success means that the people around me get to be successful in their chosen fields. When they are doing well, I do well too. As the saying goes, "A rising tide lifts all boats."

Building trust-based relationships is a key ingredient to success. People like to work with people they like and trust. I always look up and reach out to people that I perceive to be doing much better than me. They may have better connections, are better educated, or are very successful in their fields. Successful people are usually willing to share their knowledge and experience with others. I also feel successful when respected members of my community look up to me for guidance and value my opinion and input.

The best success of all, though, comes from the success of my clients. I will never forget the time our teams had worked with a client for months on an electoral system in South Africa. While watching the election updates on the television, I saw an elderly lady sitting in a wheelbarrow, being pushed by a youthful man toward a voting booth. It felt so good to have been part of enabling that elderly lady to vote, and that the client was happy with the results of our efforts. Success means that my clients are valuing working with me and that I am attaining a "Trusted Advisor" status.

You can achieve so much more when you surround yourself with successful people.

You can't do this on your own. It is about the people!

"Without consultation, plans are frustrated, But with many counsellors they succeed."

— PROVERBS 15:22

Sharing and Giving

Success means I can share what I have with others and expect nothing in return. I can inspire, lift, support, and improve the lives of others so they, too, can achieve their own successes.

I am involved in several social community projects and fundraisers, and it gives me immense pleasure when we can rally other community members and successfully achieve our set targets. It was through my involvement with one of these community projects that I discovered I had some fundraising skills. Success, for me, then became gaining the confidence to pick up the phone, pitch a worthwhile philanthropic project, and get people to buy into it and open their wallets. Now *that* feels good!

Never Stop Learning

I am a serial student. There is so much to learn. I set aside time each day for attending online courses, mastermind communities, webinars, research, and reading. I am a voracious reader. I read anything I can lay my hands on. I go through an average of one book a week—though I would like to bump that up to two books a week. I am a member of several book clubs. I subscribe to an audiobooks service and use my commute time to listen to audiobooks. I record my material, too. I also conduct a lot of training, coaching, and mentoring of others. Writing and teaching forces me to be on top of all the new trends and thinking out in the marketplace. I invest a lot in my self-development.

> *"This says the Lord, the God of Israel: Write all the words that I have spoken to you in a book."*
>
> — *JEREMIAH* 30:2

Success Means Winning

Success means winning. It means making a sale. It means gaining new clients. It means fighting off a negative mindset. It means having meaningful relationships. It means sharing.

And while we're at it, I want to make loads of money, too.

Success is About Faith

One has to believe that, in whatever we do, we need to commit our plans and work to the Lord. He will guide us through them.

> *"For I know the plans I have for you, plans to prosper you and not to harm you, plans to give you hope and a future."*
>
> — *JEREMIAH* 29:11

Success means different things to different people. Writing this chapter has helped crystalize in my mind what success means to me. Am I done yet? No. My chosen path is still under construction. I am not done yet.

Just like the battle my mama had with the king cobra snake, I want to keep on fighting, working hard, and winning. She won. I can win, too.

You can reach Monica at monicarubombora.com.

26

PASSIONIZE YOUR PERSONAL BRAND

SOFIA JARLO

We all want success, don't we? The bigger the better. But we need to build it.

If I had to summarize my best success tips into one single word, I would choose the word "alignment." It has been a game changer for me, and hopefully it will help you, too, on your journey toward success. It matters what you believe, what you do, and what you think, because *that* is what manifests. Now I'd like to share some of my best insights from my path to success so you can also play the game of alignment in order to reach the top.

Follow the passion and start now!

I'm Sofia Jarlo and I know two things : life is short, and it's meant to be lived to the fullest. This insight came from the pain I felt when I lost my father in a car accident. I began to think about life. What would he have wanted? Would he have wanted to see me in pain, walking around suffering, or would he have wanted me to do some-thing? Of course he would have wanted me to fulfill my dreams, so I did. This is what I want for you, too—not to go through a loved one's death, of course, but to wake up and follow your passion and your dreams. Become the person you've always wanted to be, because that's the person you are.

"I have always wanted to know who you are!"

In 2017, an eleven-year-old came forward to talk to me after a talk I had given as part of an "author visit" at his school. The same school, in fact, I had worked at ten years before as a teacher. It turned out that his brother was one of my former pupils. Then it occurred to me that he was the little baby boy with almost no hair. The memory of him being held with his mother or father when they came to pick up his brother came clearly in mind.

Now he stood in front of me and said something that puzzled me: "I've always wanted to know who you are!"

I smiled. I had the same question for myself. I winked at him and replied, "Now you know!"

But did I really know myself? I had managed the school visits that I did in my new role as a writer. Initially, I thought it was all about my book, but it turned out to be more than that. The pupils were honestly curious about who I was. So, I dug deeper and got to know myself on a whole other level. This knowledge led me to successfully plan and master my personal brand. Several insights came along the way that made me realize both what I had been missing and what I had created. I became the role model I had been missing in my life.

People can feel intentions

The boy's question made me think. I knew I had a good reputation, but I didn't think people would still be talking about me ten years after I'd finished teaching and moved away. After a lot of analysis, I came up with two reasons why they were. The first is that people can feel your intentions. My intentions when teaching were not only to follow the rules and try to hit my goals, but to create a good atmosphere for others to grow. I thought if I could make my pupils have a positive mindset, their ability to learn would increase. Secondly, a real impact is made through feelings. People remember how you made them feel.

Align with your purpose

One of the main things you need to do is to become aware of and certain of your deepest "why." So, are you aware of it? If you are, then you have something great to consciously build on. If not, search for your own way to find it. It's like peeling an onion, layer by layer. When you reach the source, you'll know, and you'll enjoy knowing your purpose for the rest of your life.

When you are aware of your "why," the whole game changes. You gain an advantage beyond your wildest dreams. Suddenly you can strategically align yourself and your business with your purpose on a conscious level and make sure what you say, think, believe, and do go in that direction—the direction of success.

Believe and be ready to fight

When I managed to get my books into the museum, my colleagues asked me: "How did you do that?" The truth is, I didn't see a limitation. Why wouldn't they accept my high-quality, self-published fiction books for kids at the museum? I already knew what kids thought about the books, as hundreds had read them already, so I wasn't worried about what adults would think. I think if you believe in your product, you will feel more certain about your decisions. Your enthusiasm will show others what to think.

Develop the craft, the game, and your business with smart people

Don't ever make the mistake of thinking you are the most clever person on the playground! Be brave enough to hang out with colleagues who are smarter, funnier, and more knowledgeable than you and you'll evolve. Do you hang out with people in your business who help you improve your work? It's the era of the "doer," where connecting with other people has never been easier. Take advantage of it!

Love to listen!

Listening is underrated. So is asking for help. People want to help. They want to listen to what others are saying. When I was a little girl, I was often criticized in school for not being a "talker," but times have changed. Being a natural listener is now one of my best and most prized skills. Be eager to learn and care! When you listen, you also calm your mind. When your mind is calm, there's room for thinking and you can get insights more easily. First and foremost, though, never forget to listen to yourself. Ask your inner self questions. The answer will come. It's already out there, waiting for you. Find it!

Lessons from the past

I'm not kidding when I tell people that some of the toughest lessons I've learned have come from my own childhood. People say you shouldn't blame your childhood, but I say, "What should we blame if not our childhood?!" If you can blame it, you're in luck, because then you know where to begin your treasure hunt for who you truly are. There are many hidden clues in your childhood. The worst thing that could happen is that you'll probably emerge from your hunt wiser and braver than ever—and we want that, don't we?

Let your life story contribute to your success

Life stories are a very powerful tool. Sometimes new insights occur during the writing process and personal transformation happens, but it's not about change. You don't have to change. It is your story that changes into another tone in your own inner universe, because you get another perspective or a deeper understanding of yourself. When your perspective and understanding change, your feelings do, too, and your attitude changes in a natural way without it having to be forced. It is your attitude toward life that decides what kind of life you get. When you work with your life story you can create magic, whether you're aiming for a bestselling book or you're trying to achieve a deeper understanding of yourself to gain advantage in your business.

Storytelling touches us deeply

Did you know that storytelling is a "brain-thing?" I'm happy to tell you that a lot of research is going on right now, and we know more than ever before. Since we can prove that storytelling affects and speaks to our brains in so many more ways than we previously thought, why not use it as the power tool it is? It can be used for everything, from marketing to healing.

Today, there's an association similar to "Doctors Without Borders" called "Storytellers Without Borders." Its members visit prisons and refugee camps all over the world with a mission to tell stories to ease people's minds. Isn't that amazing? Storytelling has also been used in therapy programs around the globe for years. It's time to bring your stories forward and make your storytelling shine!

Time

One strange thing my father said to me when I was a little girl was, "Time is money." It was impossible to understand. Being a deep thinker, I tried to figure out what he meant, but I was unable to find an answer that made sense. Today, though, I have my own interpretation. Time is *like* a currency, because what you "feed your mind" with is what you might get results from. What do you let your mind spend time on? Our success often depends on what we *choose* to focus on and *what we do* with our time. Do you worry a lot? How much time do you spend worrying? Are you doing something that produces the opposite effect to what you want? Take charge of your mind and decide how you direct it and what you give attention. Make sure to spend your time on healthy, positive things that you want for yourself, your family, and your business.

Work on your vibe

When did you last focus on your "vibe?" This is surprisingly easy to do, although many people know very little about it. I myself have been amazed at how powerful words can be. For several years, I volunteered at a Red Cross call center for children and young people in Sweden and received calls from many youngsters who felt bad. I learned that we can do wonders with our choice of words. A sentence can change someone's life forever. A conversation can save someone's life. But, we can also make *ourselves* feel better by focusing on the things we love. It is important to be creative and find what you like. Write quotes that cheer you up. Words you need just for that day. Do you have any favorite words? Use them. Let them create the vibes around you. Enjoy and have fun with yourself! Let yourself be guided by what you like and it will increase your energy and make you feel good. Maybe it's words, maybe it's art, dance, or music. Maybe it's a mix of all of them. Make your own mixture of good vibes and make sure to give it a little attention every day. It will do wonders for your soul!

Use all of you

Have you reached the OMG level of your personal brand and become the entrepreneur you always wanted to be? If so, I congratulate you on your success. If not, something wonderful is waiting for you—if you play your cards right. Use all of you, in your own creative, holistic way, and don't let anything stop you. Do you want to be unstoppable?

The only way no one will be able to compete with you is if you forge your own path.

Good luck on your way to becoming unstoppable, and don't forget: "I have always wanted to know who you are." That's the insane impact level you want to reach. And if I can do it, so can you!

You can reach Sofia at sofiajarlo.com.

27

THE FLYING EAGLE FORMULA

DEB CANJA

What the Chicago Cubs and Summer Camp Taught Me About Parenting Success

In 1908, the Chicago Cubs won the World Series and then went on a losing streak of 108 years. For 71 of those years, the losses were blamed on The Curse of the Billy Goat, placed on the team in 1945 by the owner of the Billy Goat Tavern when he was asked to leave Wrigley Field because the odor of his pet goat was bothering fans. But even that curse could not overcome the success that finally brought home the championship in 2016.

Not many of us are trying to coach a baseball team to a championship, but a lot of us are raising and coaching kids, and we'd all like to protect them from a losing streak. These streaks could show up as a lack of confidence, lack of friends, trouble in school or in holding a job, divorce, depression, or substance abuse.

To be fair, the Cubs did win their division a few times. But they lost, and kept on losing, the National League Championship and the World Series. Life can also be like that, with enough good times to keep us going but the happiness of dreams fulfilled, a great career, great friends, a great marriage, and a sense of purpose—in other words, the World Series of Life—can seem out of reach.

But it doesn't have to be. By understanding the catalyst that finally brought the championship to the Cubs, we can bring the Championship of Life to our kids.

Why most parenting advice won't lead to success

What was the secret that broke the Curse of the Billy Goat? It wasn't technique. The Cubs had won their division thirteen times; they knew how to play ball. And it wasn't the players—they were good enough to get to the championships. We can't blame it on the equipment. They had the best. And over 108 years there were enough different referees that you can't chalk it up to bad refs.

Isn't that a lot like the obstacles our kids face? We wonder, are they in the right peer group? Do they have the right teacher? The right books, electronics, clothes, friends, lucky breaks?

When my boys were young, I read up on technique in magazine articles like "25 Ways To Teach Your Child To Think," and "How To Raise Kids Right: Advice From 5 Experts." I moved to a good school district and enrolled them in afterschool activities. They did chores. We ate dinner together. They had the right equipment, such as computers and books. And overall, the referees, their teachers, were good, too. But I learned, just like with the Chicago Cubs, the real key is something else.

The "success building" formula that worked for the Cubs

The Curse of the Billy Goat started to crack in 2014. That was the year the Cubs hired a new manager, Joe Maddon. He was quirky and personable and in 2015 brought a flamingo, penguin, sloth, and baby snow leopard into the clubhouse to hang out with the team. That year they won a playoff spot. In 2016, the team wore T-shirts with Maddon's advice, "Try not to suck." It became their unofficial slogan.

And that was the year the Curse was broken. The Cubs won the National League Championship *and* the World Series.

Maddon understood the "something else" that makes the difference. It's not knowledge, technique, equipment, or even the right environment. It's a mindset. Leadership is all about the mindset you help other people believe about themselves. A good mindset unleashes the ability to do extraordinary work.

There is a specific way to build this mindset, but good intentions are not enough. We need to combine good intentions with a specific, proven plan based on the *one* thing that makes the difference. That's because human beings seem hard-wired to focus on short-comings. Every mistake, every less-than-expected outcome, every failure to live up to our own (or someone else's) expectations can lead to self-blame, stress, anger, and a freezing up of that powerful belief that tells us, "I can do it."

What Maddon understood is that a good dose of fun takes away self-blame. It reframes our experience. For the Cubs, baseball became a game again, a game the players enjoyed, a game they knew how to win.

This reframing is the secret to parenting success.

Lessons from Summer Camp

In 1956, my parents bought property on a lake in Northern Michigan and started Camp Flying Eagle (CFE), a summer camp for boys. It was my dad's dream to reframe a boy's opinion of himself by helping him create what we now call "a success mindset." He wanted to teach the approach that made it possible for him to survive a difficult childhood.

Orphaned at the age of eleven, my father was sent to live at the YMCA. Through discipline and hard work he earned an athletic scholarship to the University of Michigan, where he went on to become an All-American diver and swimmer. With a master's degree in education, he went on to become a teacher and a coach.

But my father had an even bigger dream: to share his knowledge about what a boy needs to build a successful life. That was the mission of CFE and the unique program we now call "The Flying Eagle Formula." Over a period of twenty-seven years, over 3,000 young boys went through the camp and experienced the Formula.

In 2019 we captured that Formula and explained how and why it works in the book, *Swim the Lake Before You Row the Boat: Awaken a Boy's Success Mindset, Unleash His Confidence and Give Him the Foundation for a Great Life*. Ever since, we've been asked, what about girls? The good news is that the principles are universal and work for girls, too. And for adults. But we focused on boys because we've seen more than sixty years of amazing results when the formula is applied to boys.

Over and over the men—who came to CFE as boys—went on to have wonderful and rewarding lives as great husbands, amazing fathers, successful businessmen, and appreciated community leaders. Many became teachers. They said that the success mindset they learned at CFE had put them on the path to success.

What is a success mindset? It is a specific set of core beliefs that are so powerful they attract financial, spiritual, social, emotional, and relationship success into life. At the heart of it is the rock-solid belief that "I can do it. I can succeed at whatever I put my mind to." It also includes these additional beliefs:

- People like and respect me,
- I can be responsible for myself,
- Other people believe I can be responsible for myself,
- I bring happiness to others,
- My life matters and there is a purpose for my being here.

These core beliefs are the greatest gift we can give our kids (and ourselves).

How or why does it work? One theory is that when we focus our mind on a goal, we naturally begin to prepare ourselves to reach that goal by doing things that will move us closer to it. We also program ourselves to look for opportunities that will help us get there. It means that we make our success by focusing on it and working at it.

Another theory says that everything in the world is made of vibrating energy and that this energy is shaped into physical matter by our individual and collective thoughts. These thoughts vibrate at different frequencies, and frequencies that are similar "find each other" in order to be in harmony. The deepest beliefs we hold about ourselves vibrate and attract the thoughts and actions of other people that are of the same frequency. Some people call that The Law of Attraction. The Bible says, "You reap what you sow." In other words, your thoughts create the reality you live in.

Our experience shows that once you hold powerful core beliefs about who you are, they attract situations that validate what you *already believe* about yourself. It is at that point that your focus on a goal and your preparation will create success from the opportunities that come to you. However, without those powerful core beliefs, nothing really turns out as you hope it will. That's why our Formula focuses on what a child believes about himself. It brings "Law of Attraction" principles to parenting.

It also means you are creating the future right now, in the present, because whatever beliefs and feelings you hold now about yourself will bring more of the same in the future. The people and situations will change, but your feelings will be the same. America's most successful people, from millionaires and billionaires to spiritual masters, have used this understanding to bring happiness, meaning, money, and fulfillment into their lives. The Flying Eagle Formula provides an easy way to apply it to help a child.

Easy ways to build a success mindset in a child

The hardest part of building a success mindset in a child is getting the adults to keep the goal front and center, to stay focused on the *one* thing that makes the difference: what a child believes about him or herself. With that in mind, here are three easy strategies that will work, *if* you keep that *one* thing clearly in mind.

"I can do it!"

The cornerstone belief that "I can do it!" most often comes from experiencing success and then forming the belief that "I am a successful person." Your job is to find opportunities that lead to that belief.

What is your child good at? What are his or her strengths? What does he or she *like* to do? This is not a time to pick activities or skills that you think your child "should" have. Instead, find things that a child *wants* to do and at which, with effort, he or she *can be* successful.

What are three different likes or strengths your child has? For each, think of a creative way for him or her to experience success using that strength. Then think of how you might recognize and celebrate the accomplishment. For example, if your son loves to tell jokes, give him the opportunity to write a joke book with at least three jokes. If he's reluctant, suggest he could earn 10¢ from you for each word written (my dad used to pay me a nickel per word). Celebrate by sharing the finished book with family and friends. Does he like building things? Can he build a LEGO creation you can display? If your daughter loves to draw, ask if she'd design a family greeting card. Does your child like math? Give her $100 imaginary dollars to invest and trade in the stock market and pay (in real dollars) any profit she makes over the $100.

Get thoughtful, get creative, and remember that you want your child to come to *know*, through successful experiences, that he or she *can* tackle something new and *succeed*.

"People like me and believe in me."

At CFE, the adult staff often sat at an outdoor patio to read the paper. Boys were welcome to sit and talk or read with the staff. On the patio they shared their opinions about current events and camp happenings. The adults listened, they discussed, and they respected the boys' opinions. In those interactions was an important message: *your views are important, and we like talking with you.*

Every day presents new opportunities to share that message—and it starts young. The younger the better. Remember, the content of what is being discussed is not the most important topic. The most important topic is the hidden message you are sending; the one that says "I like you. I like spending time with you. I like talking with you. I respect your opinions."

Another easy way to send that message is by honoring a child's choice over personal matters, such as what to wear. When you let a person choose something for himself, you are telling him that you believe he can be responsible for himself and that you have faith in his judgment.

"I have a purpose, a place, and a reason for being here. I am needed."

The feeling of self-worth we get when others value our contribution is powerful. It creates a mental and emotional picture of being needed, of having something important to share, and of feeling valued. That picture creates a future, as does the past. That's why you want to commit now to finding opportunities for your child to experience a feeling and belief of belonging and of knowing that his contribution matters. You want him to know there is a purpose and reason for him to be here—that he *can* make a difference, that he *does* make a difference, and that his value is *recognized by others.*

How? Whenever you do a project or task or chore *together,* you create a team and a sense of belonging. When you help others, you make a difference. Is there something at home that needs to be fixed? Can you take the time to include the children you love in the effort? Is there a project in your community that needs volunteers? Can you visit seniors in assisted living, do craft activities with folks in memory care, serve food at a soup kitchen, collect toys or books for homeless kids? All those and more can give a child the powerful message that he *can* make a difference, that his life *does* have meaning, and that his efforts *are* appreciated. The future rewards are far beyond what you can now imagine.

Keep your focus on the ONE thing that matters

Every child can have a success mindset. Their circumstances might be different, their challenges might be different, but they can all have, do, and be amazing. No matter what age a child is now, from babies to toddlers to teens, what he believes about himself is the single greatest factor in determining his happiness, his confidence, his ability to make friends, his willingness to try new things, and his ability to take responsibility for himself.

By making a success mindset the most important goal of parenting, we *can* create happy, empowered, success-mindset kids.

You can connect with Deb at www.spencerwhitepublishing.com

28

A COMMITMENT TO GIVING

ANTHONY COSTA

What I'm about to share with you is NOT theory. It works. More importantly, it will work for you just as it's worked for thousands of my previous clients.

So please keep an open mind as we proceed together. We're going to dismantle some beliefs that are holding you back and replace them with truths that will help you succeed.

Now, let's get right to it... There are three major false beliefs keeping you from achieving and retaining your goals. The worst of these is the belief in *Lack, Not Enough Of,* or, in a word, *Scarcity*.

Scarcity, thinking you are not enough, or that you don't have enough, time, money, love, energy, creativity, etc. is behind most (if not, all) crimes, ethical and moral violations, even wars.

It's also been proven, at least since the 1950's, that you cannot act contrary to your beliefs. Because of that, let's take a closer look at the false belief of Scarcity by asking a question...

Q. If a thief had all the money he or she needed, and if he or she was secure that more money would always be there, would he or she still feel a need to steal?
A. Probably not!

I said, "probably" because our thief may still want to experience the thrill, the adrenaline rush he or she gets from planning, risking, pulling off, and reaping the rewards of a theft.

But if we look closer at that motivation, we'll see the thief is still coming from scarcity. Only now, it's not the fear of lack of money, it's the fear of not having enough excitement.

Can you see how this works and how it holds you back? If you're not quite sure, allow me to further explain.

In addition to not being able to act contrary to our beliefs, whether those beliefs are positive or negative, we also have conscious and unconscious goals.

Unfortunately, the unconscious goals are often at cross-purposes to, and often override, our conscious goals. Because of this, we stay stuck and fail to achieve the goals we consciously work on.

So what's all this have to do with "A Commitment To Giving"?

Just this...

When you make a "commitment to giving" and then follow through with action every chance you get, you are reminding yourself that scarcity is not real. You're acknowledging that it's nothing more than a false belief that was instilled in you by caring, but unknowing people since you were a child (which, by the way, is the reason why *it's not your fault* for not yet reaching your goals).

Now, if I were sitting where you are, I might be thinking, *"But wait, I do have a lack, a scarcity of money, or love, or time, or energy or creativity. How then, is it only a belief?"*

Great question!

So let's explore the idea of a false belief right now, and dismantle it once and for all. As an example, let's use M-O-N-E-Y!

We hear it all the time... *"There is not enough money to go around. The rich people have it all. I don't have enough."*

But remember, since you cannot act contrary to your beliefs, and since you get what you focus on, and since you're usually focusing on your lack of money, that's what you get, more "lack" of money.

But here are some life-altering facts you're probably not aware of...

In the U.S. alone, three trillion dollars (that's "trillion" with a "T") pass through our Federal Reserve System every day!

Another three trillion is passed hand to hand by things being bought and sold throughout the country. Everything from buying your Saturday night pizza - to the millions of transactions that occur online every single day.

That's a total of SIX TRILLION DOLLARS A DAY! Plus, another six trillion dollars passes through our Forex system, the foreign currency exchange, also every day!

That means *twelve trillion dollars are* floating around, every day, in the U.S. alone. We're not even talking about the rest of the world.

So there's no shortage, or scarcity, of money in the world! Period! And... *It's Your World!*

Let that sink in for a moment, It's Your World. Here's proof. If we take you out of this world, then it no longer exists - not for you anyway.

This scarcity belief applies to everything else that's beneficial as well. Take "Love" for example: With almost eight billion people in the world, do you *really* believe there is no one out there for you? If you do, it's just one more example of you coming from false beliefs (scarcity and others) that you were tragically exposed to, and indoctrinated with as a child!

Just stop and think... Eight billion to one! Don't you think there could be someone out there for you?

Here's the point: There's no scarcity of money, love, time, energy, creativity, or any else beneficial. The only reason you haven't experienced this truth, this reality, is because you were taught to operate from a false belief that it's a world of "not enough of" and scarcity!

Earlier, I asked you to please keep an open mind because I knew we would be using facts to dismantle some false beliefs that you have been holding dear to you.

You see, even though they're not true, false beliefs are often precious to you because of where and when you were taught them, and more importantly, because of who unwittingly taught them to you.

Because of that, negative circumstances and situations were created that you've become very familiar and comfortable with. This makes it extremely difficult to let go of your false beliefs.

But, here's a helpful secret...

All growth, all advancement in life comes from stepping outside your "comfort zone". Sadly, few people learn to enjoy being outside their comfort zone long enough to gain the benefits of doing so. Their inner dialogue goes something like this: *"Sure it worked for other people, but it won't work for me. Nothing ever does, no matter how hard I try."*

But... You are NOT the same person you were five years ago, or last year, or even yesterday.

As Tony Robbins says, "All the moments of your past, do not equal one moment of now!" Actually, I think Confucius said it first, a long, long time ago.

Which means... If you're thinking what we're discussing will work for others, but not for you, then it's just another false belief that you were unwittingly taught by well-meaning, misguided people. These truths work and they'll work for you too.

So, start right now. Start exploring your false beliefs, in particular, "Scarcity", by making a *Commitment To Giving* as often as you can. Doing this, will help you to begin dispelling the false belief in lack and scarcity.

It doesn't cost much, or take a lot of time either. You can be kinder to the grocery store clerk with a smile. You can give away things you never use to a local charity drive. You can take time on the basketball court to help a struggling child learn to play.

Start breaking down your false belief in scarcity whenever it raises its ugly head, and focus on abundance instead. Then, you'll start to experience just that... an abundance of time, money, love, energy, creativity, and more!

By the way, here's a great example of a false belief at work.

Before we go further, I'd like to share an excellent illustration of not being able to act contrary to our beliefs, even when they're completely false.

Let's say we were at a live, in-person seminar. The speaker shares a little about his personal life and tells us that he absolutely loves cats, but is terrified of dogs. Even the tiniest little dog totally frightens him.

Let's further say the setting on stage is like a cozy living room, with a hardwood floor, a nice woven carpet, a comfy sofa with matching chairs, and beautiful plants all around.

So, the speaker is sharing his love for cats, when he sees something under the sofa and says, "Oh, cool. Look, there's a Persian cat over there., I can see its furry tail." He rushes over to the sofa, gets down on one knee, reaches out to pet the cat, when suddenly...

The animal spins around and starts barking because it's really a tiny dog!

The speaker then runs off-stage, screaming, *"Ahhhhh! It's a dog! Get it away from me!"*

Now let's take a really close look at this situation.

What was the truth about the animal? Well, the truth is, it was always a dog. However, what did the speaker (falsely) believe it was? He believed it was a cat, and how did he respond to the animal?

He reacted to it as if it were a cat, because that's what he *believed* in spite of the truth. Only *after* he received overwhelming data, the "real facts", did the speaker react to the reality that it was actually a dog all along.

You can see this from this example how limiting, and potentially dangerous operating from false briefs can be? Think about it. What if the dog wasn't a small one? What if it had a small furry tail, but it was a huge, ill-tempered, mean-spirited dog? What if it liked to attack?!

Get the picture? Your false beliefs hurt you, and hold you back all the time.

So, start training yourself to question whether or not, at any given time, you are operating from the false belief of scarcity, or any other incorrect beliefs that were instilled in you.

Oh, and speaking of questioning, there is an interesting, but potentially damaging, phenomenon that occurs in our western culture (and maybe other cultures too, but definitely in western societies).

That phenomenon is one in which we always want *the answer.* But, did you know that questions are far more powerful and can help you a lot more than answers? It's actually true, except when it comes to achieving and retaining our goals. Then, one specific question is very limiting, even harmful, and that question is... *"Will I succeed?"*

That question paralyzes us. It freezes our creative flow because for most of us, the overwhelming amount of challenges and tasks we will have to endure in order to accomplish our goals can be, and often is, terrifying.

A much more empowering question to ask is, *"After I achieve my goal, then what?"* In other words, after you achieve that goal, then what bigger, more important goal will you go for next?

By asking questions like that, your subconscious mind starts to align your unconscious goals with your conscious goals. It looks for ways of helping you achieve the smaller, shorter-term goal in order to help you get the more important, longer-range goal.

You can jump-start all this right now by allowing yourself the luxury of questioning your beliefs, and living outside your comfort zone. That way, you can quickly begin to experience the benefits of taking the right type of risks.

Now, we're not talking about crazy, over-the-top, reckless risks, like betting you can dress up in an all-black ninja suit and stand on an unlit street at night and not get hit by a car.

Get it? We are not talking about taking crazy, reckless risks!

Instead, we're talking about calculated risks where you've carefully weighed the pros and cons, and where there are lots of pros on your side of the table while the cons are kept to a minimum.

Those are the types of risks we're talking about, and those are the types of risks you can start taking once you begin questioning things and start habitually living outside your comfort zone.

A Word of Caution Regarding Your Family & Friends...

Although most of us have family and friends who truly love us, many of them are actually afraid of us succeeding. The reason for their fear is because it mirrors back to them what is truly possible, and more importantly for them, what they are *not* doing.

Since most folks want to stay with what they know, with what's comfortable, seeing you stepping outside of your comfort zone can be a very unpleasant experience for them.

This unpleasant experience only intensifies for them the more you achieve success. So, please be careful when you begin questioning your belief systems, living outside your comfort zone, and reaching your goals.

Often, the people we think will be most happy for us won't be. It's not because they don't want to, or that they love us less, or that they are jealous of our new success. No, it's only because they're running up against their own false beliefs, and "that" can be a very, very scary thing.

Hopefully, you won't experience this with your friends and family, but be aware it can, and often does, happen. If it does, please be kind with your thoughts toward them and remember just how frightened, and how stuck in their own false beliefs they still are.

However, do not let any of that stop you. Your happiness is as important as anyone's, and you deserve, and are entitled to, all the riches life has to offer.

You can begin bringing those riches to yourself today by dismantling the strongest foe you've encountered this far in life... *the false belief in scarcity*. You can defeat it by proclaiming a deep, sincere, **Commitment To Giving**.

In fact, here's a proclamation for you. By the way, proclamations are much different from affirmations. Affirmations generally do not work because your mind knows what you're saying is not yet true and it rebels. So saying, "I am a millionaire." when you're not, will make your mind say, "That's not true!", and then it shuts down on you.

By contrast, a Proclamation is simply a statement, to yourself and to the universe, of what you are promising to do. With that in mind, as soon as you've got a moment to yourself, literally stand up and proclaim out loud the following:

> "Here and Now", at this exact moment, I proclaim that I will "give" as often as I can, in as many ways as I can, to as many people as I can. By doing this, I will remove my old indoctrination, retrain myself, and dismantle my false beliefs in lack and scarcity. I am further acknowledging to myself and the universe that it is an abundant world, and that I am now starting to allow that abundance to flow to me in a successful manner.

(It helps if you repeat the above proclamation as often as you can each day).

That's it for now my friends.. Thanks for being so incredibly brave, and thanks for keeping an open mind about this new journey you're embarking on. I feel privileged and very *lucky* to have shared this time with you.

I wish each and every one of you, the very Best of Luck as well.. You certainly deserve it.

Peace and Blessings,

Anthony Costa

You can connect with Anthony at LinkedIn.com/in/4anthonycosta.

JOIN US

Like what you have read here? You can help change the world too. Here are three things you can do.

Leave a review here:
https://review.raybrehm.com/tsc
or a video review
https://review.raybrehm.com/tscvideo

Join us at the Success Code Summit.
https://www.successcodesummit.com

Join one of our upcoming anthology books like *The Success Code.*
https://www.co-author.me

Made in the USA
Coppell, TX
21 September 2020